A Long Way From St Petersburg

The Tom Conway Story

C E PARKINSON

A Long Way From St Petersburg.

The Tom Conway Story

Second Edition

Copyright © 2016 C E Parkinson

All rights reserved.

ISBN: 10:1516868447
ISBN-13:978-1516868445

Front cover: Tom Conway publicity photo circa 1942 – photographer unknown.

Fig 1 Stock photo intended for advertising circa 1944
Figs 2 and 3 photographed by C E Parkinson 2014 ©
Figs 3, 4 and 7 subject to licence obtained from PA Images

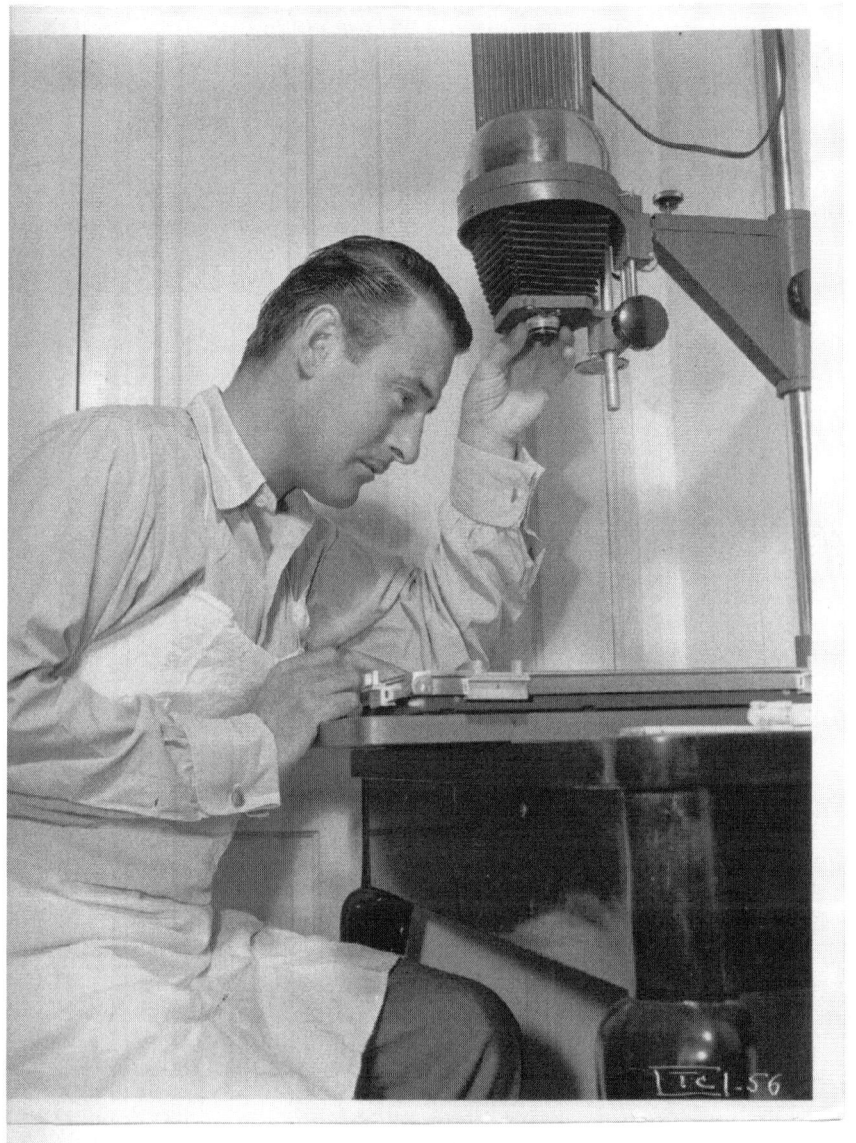
Fig 1: Tom Conway at home. Photograph intended for advertising. Circa 1944

CONTENTS

Acknowledgments

Preface   1

1   "Our parents played no favourites"   7
2   "Stick up your hands"   17
3   "I had plenty of rope"   22
4   "I was a good type"   26
5   Hollywood 1940 - 1942   30
6   The RKO Years 1942 - 1946   35
7   The Falcon flies the coop   51
8   His career is dying a natural death   58
9   A yearning for the bachelor life   63
10   Tom refused to give up   74
11   Broke and ailing   79
12   Post Script   83

Filmography

Works cited

"I am a man who has done many things. I've been a soldier, a gambler, a war correspondent. I've no rheumatism, no patience and no money..."

– Tom Conway, as Tom Lawrence in *The Falcon Strikes Back*.

ACKNOWLEDGMENTS

My thanks to Pat McDougall for all his invaluable help and for permission to use excerpts from *Ramblings of an also Ran*. Material located in Australian newspapers on Trove website has been used courtesy of the National Library of Australia.

Preface

I am a man who has done many things. I've been a rancher, a miner, a bus driver, an engineer, a boat builder, a salesman and an actor. I've got no money and have some patience. (What Tom Conway may have said if asked to sum up his working life.)

Who was Tom Conway many people may ask today? Even if they do not instantly recognise his name, or have never seen any of his films, there is a strong possibility that unknowingly, they have heard his delightfully precise and resonant voice before. They may have listened to a distinctively refined, Englishman's voice on the radio, as a narrator of a film or a voice over for a character in a Disney film and wondered who it was. I know because that is what happened to me. I had seen *Waterloo Bridge* (1940) starring Robert Taylor and Vivien Leigh a number of times and had wondered who the narrator was. I would watch the film waiting for that person to appear or see his name in the credits but he was not credited. The narrator was Tom Conway. Ironically, I later discovered that he had played a small part in the film.

Similarly, how many people have seen Disney's *Peter Pan* (1953) and wondered who narrated it. It was Tom Conway. A similar thing happened some years ago when I was watching a re-run of the western TV show, *Rawhide*, on TCM. It was the *Incident of the Tumbleweed* (1959) where an English actor plays the evil murderer, Sinclair. Having been an avid film buff since a teenager back in the 1960's and having seen many vintage Hollywood films over the years I felt I should know this actor and yet I had no idea to his identity. His accent was far too striking and precise for him to be an American imitating an English accent. I did not watch the credits at the end of the show, the moment was gone and I forgot all about him. Again, the unknown actor I later discovered was Tom Conway.

Then one summer, a few years back, I was hard at work writing my first book. I had the TV on but was not watching it – just listening. The BBC was showing a black and white film series starring George Sanders as Gay Lawrence aka 'The Falcon'. I had never seen the 'Falcon' series before. Two 'Falcon' films were shown daily around lunchtime and I tuned in religiously. For some reason my attention was drawn to the TV when George Sanders was lying in bed with his head bandaged, he was speaking but his lips were not moving. It sounded a bit like Sanders but it was not him because the voice was warmer. Then the camera showed a dark haired, handsome man with a pencil thin moustache concealed behind a curtain. He was the person who was speaking. The film was *The Falcon's Brother* (1942).

From that moment, I was hooked on the series because the person whose voice had attracted my attention, I soon discovered, was George Sanders' real-life brother, Tom Conway. Conway I noted straightaway had an enthusiasm about him and kindly humour that Sanders did not possess. In sharp contrast Sanders came over as patronising and smarmy. I needed to find out more about Conway, why I had never heard of him and why his name had been forgotten over the years and what had happened to him?

During my research I asked a number of more mature people if they remembered Tom Conway. Of those who said they did most added that he worked in the shadows of his more famous brother. I had to find out then the reason why Tom did not become a more celebrated actor.

I soon discovered that Tom Conway was not very different in real life from the 'Falcon' character that he portrayed in the 1940's. He was a handsome, suave, debonair, immaculately dressed and likeable man. His poise and manners were impeccable and his big friendly smile and humour helped to make him a favourite with his contemporaries and the press.

Like the 'Falcon', Conway had many professions throughout his working life. Similarly, like his feathered friend, he had many adventures and sometimes-hilarious and embarrassing situations to disentangle himself from. Tom Conway appears to have been the kind of person who, if marooned alone on an uninhabited island, could still get into trouble.

From the beginning of his Hollywood career, Tom believed that he was best suited to playing sophisticated comedic or romantic roles similar to the ones he had played on the English stage in the 1930's e.g. *'Private Lives'* [1] by Noel Coward. He would mention this fact many times during his acting career as he became increasingly frustrated with being type cast as 'The Falcon'.

[1] Tom Conway played the part of Victor in *Private Lives* a play adapted for radio with Lawrence Olivier and Vivien Leigh in 1940.

RKO bosses told him his name was not big enough when he asked them why they did not cast him in 'A' pictures. After all, they were paying his wages and he was at his most successful and profitable for them when playing a detective in 'B' movies. Tom could see their point but he was finding it increasingly difficult to hide his frustration.

Tom Conway was a perfectionist who had an underlying, deep-seated fear of having to start all over again as an actor. He confessed to not wanting to have to take the parts of butlers and elevator attendants again. Nonetheless, his working life was full of fresh starts as he regenerated his career repeatedly over the years.

In his early days in Hollywood, he came across as a shy and self-conscious actor. However, once he had made the transition from stage to movie actor and became more experienced he overcame that initial shyness which may have been his English reserve. He was patient with new actors and helped them as much as he could because he understood what they were going through.

To his chagrin, as previously mentioned, he had a famous younger brother, George Sanders, to contend with. At first, having a celebrated actor for a brother who he resembled and sounded like assisted his career but eventually it became his nemesis. After all, there was only one George Sanders. Tom wanted recognition as a good actor in his own right and hated to trade on his brother's name. He was envious of his brother's stature and try as he may he could not emulate it.

Sadly by 1960, this once handsome, charming, versatile and athletic actor had been battling terminal liver disease, with related life threatening and life changing complications, for at least seven years. It is believed that his heavy drinking, which according to friends did not affect his acting, eventually led to his illness. Tom admitted that he drank a lot but did not believe he had a problem with it.

Unfortunately, Mr Conway is no longer with us. This year, 2014, he would have celebrated his 110th birthday. He would have made a great interviewee because he was always amiable and friendly towards members of the media. Would he have told all? He liked to tell a story but he was also very loyal to his family and friends. It is also regretful that his close family, friends and peers are also not available to interview.

In order to try to discover the rise and decline of this genial and humorous man's career it was necessary to use all vital biographical material available in the form of newspapers, periodicals and books. Ancestral sources were used to fill in the gaps in his antecedents, which takes the reader on a journey from St Petersburg, Russia back to 17th century Dundee, Scotland. With the lack of a first account interview from the main subject it was necessary to find out what the social and economic conditions were like in the different places where he lived to try to understand what may have influenced his life and career.

Consequently there are gaps in his story and sometimes it has been necessary to glean evidence from as many sources as possible to try to fill those gaps. The problem then is that you may get conflicting pieces of evidence which need to be scrutinized carefully and viewed with caution.

Tom's life story began in imperial St Petersburg, Russia at the beginning of the 20th century. He went to England in 1915 where he was formally educated. Reference has been made to the incident with the pistol that led to his expulsion from the prestigious Bedales School. After this episode, his parents sent him to the less impressive Brighton College. We then follow his emigration to Rhodesia where he became a miner, bus driver and cattle rancher. He returned to England six years later, broke, very eager to work but still suffering from the effects of a near fatal case of malaria. We look briefly at the ten years that follow in 1930's England during the Depression where he had various occupations before becoming a stage actor and radio broadcaster.

Finally, we trail him to Hollywood just before the outbreak of WWII and see his success in getting a contract with Metro Goldwyn Mayer where he worked for two years before taking over the 'Falcon' role from his brother at RKO, which he will always be famous. He became disillusioned with the poor films he was making and very frustrated at being typecast. The story then focuses on his decision to take the free-lancing route and the decline in his film career.

After taking an eighteen-month career break, Tom returned to acting once more and he found success in television in the early 1950's as Inspector Mark Saber. His story concludes with his illnesses, battle with alcohol and frequent hospital visits before he is discovered destitute near the end of his life. Once again, after a long stint in hospital, teetotal for nearly a year and surviving on a federal pension, Tom is ready to start again at the age of 62. He has a multitude of ideas going round in his head but sadly, he becomes gravely ill again before his dreams come to fruition.

Tom Conway featured in around sixty-three pictures with leads in twenty-seven. Reports of the total number of films he appeared in range from 283 to 290. But it is believed the total includes TV, radio and stage appearances. He had a steady career and often seemed to be on the verge of real stardom but never quite made it. An appended filmography gives lists of Production Company, running time, crew and main cast for each film. A list of his known television and radio credits follow.

C E Parkinson
September 2014
England

Author's Note

In this second edition, I have updated some information and added some extra notes.

C E Parkinson
March 2016

Fig. 2: Peter and Paul Cathedral, St Petersburg 2014 (Peter and Paul Fortress)
Photograph by C.E.Parkinson

"Our parents played no favourites"
St Petersburg
1904 - 1914

Thomas Charles Sanders was born into a wealthy British family in St Petersburg, Russia on 15th September 1904. His birthplace and main family home for the first ten years was Petroffsky Ostroff No 6. His father was a wholesale rope manufacturer and his mother an eminent horticulturalist. His family enjoyed a lifestyle that many people today can only try to imagine. In those early, happy childhood years of the early twentieth century, he was blissfully unaware that in a few years' time his family would lose their home, business, many estates and fortune. (1)

Pure white, crystalline snow often adorns the rooftops of St Petersburg's many stunning churches and palaces during the long winter months. The first snow can sometimes be seen as early as October and can last until the following March. The city is only six degrees south of the Arctic Circle and it is the northern most one in the world.

St Petersburg enjoys on average, about four months of milder weather a year. The summers can be scorching but not unbearably hot. Surprisingly the humidity can be quite high. On a visit made by the author to St Petersburg in May 2013, the temperature was twenty degrees Celsius. The humidity was very high and there was a light dusting of sand covering the entire city. Notably, the wind off the Gulf of Finland can be biting even in the warmer months.

The city is well worth a visit with over one hundred museums, palaces and churches to explore. One attraction is Peter and Paul Fortress which was St Petersburg's first building. It was founded on a small island in the Neva delta on 27th May 1703 and that day became the birthday of the city. It is immediately recognisable by the amazing golden spire of St Peter and Paul Cathedral which is 122 metres high and visible all over the city centre. Housed in the cathedral are the tombs of the Russian tsars – the Romanovs. (Fig 2)

Much of the city was badly damaged during the 'Siege of Leningrad' which was a prolonged military operation undertaken by Germany during World War II. (St Petersburg's name was changed to Petrograd in 1914 and then in 1924 it was changed to Leningrad. In 1991 the city's name was changed back to St Petersburg.)The siege started on 8th September 1941, when the last road to the city was cut off. Although the Soviets managed to open a narrow land corridor to the city on 18th January 1943, the blockade was finally lifted on 27th January 1944, 872 days after it began.

Since the war, a great deal of renovation and reconstruction work has been carried out and today many of its buildings are practically back to what they were like in the tsarist days.

It was in this architecturally impressive city that Pastor A. Richie baptised Thomas Charles Sanders, eldest son of Henry Ernest Peter Sanders and Margaret Jenney Bertha Kolbe, at the British-American Congregational Church, Alexandroffsky, on 21st December 1904. A copy of the certificate was sent to the General Records Office, Somerset House, London. (2)

There are two dates recorded on Thomas' baptism certificate, 2nd and 15th September. (2) The first date being the Old Russian calendar date, which was altered after the Soviets took over Russia in 1917, the second the Gregorian calendar date. Vladimir Ilyich Lenin had agreed that the Soviet Union should fall in line with the rest of the world in using the Gregorian calendar. In addition to fix the date, the Soviets ordered that February 1st 1918 should become February 14th 1918. (3)

Cecil H. Hackie (Acting Consul) nearly four years later on 27th May 1908 subsequently registered Thomas Charles Sanders birth at the British Consulate, St Petersburg. Henry Sanders signed the entry giving his profession as 'Mill Manager'. (1) It is not clear why it took so long to register Thomas's birth because a child is normally registered within six weeks of birth. It may have just been an oversight on the Sanders' part.

Thomas Sanders had two siblings, George Henry Sanders born 3rd July 1906 and Margaret Mary Violet Sanders born 27th October 1912, both in St Petersburg. George Sanders would go on to become an award-winning Hollywood actor and Margaret Sanders an interior designer. In later years George Sanders went bankrupt and sadly committed suicide in 1972.

St Petersburg 1904

Petroffsky Ostroff/Petrovsky Ostrov or Peter's Island is a small slice of land and one of 44 islands on which St Petersburg stands. Peter the Great founded the city in 1703 on the marshy banks of the Neva River. The islands, linked by a series of canals, are crossed over by around 300 bridges. In 1705, Peter transferred the capital of Russia from Moscow to St Petersburg. Today the island is the home of the 'Petrovsky Stadium' which is the home of FC Zenit St Petersburg. The former name of the stadium, which was opened in 1925, was 'The Lenin Stadium'.

Mr H. Gibson visited St Petersburg in June 1904. He wrote a letter to relatives in Australia telling them that the city was "the most beautiful and picturesque" one he had ever seen. Furthermore the streets were "very broad" and "clean." He added that "small steamers" and boats of "every description" buzzed about in the canals all day. Gibson mentions another form of transport the "droshky" and remarks that the all the drivers wore a "number" on their backs. He describes a "big system" of horse drawn tramways where some trams were drawn by "four horses" with smaller trams driven by two. (4) Apparently there were "permanent stages" in the parks which were called "summer gardens" and bands played in the gardens and streets every night. The locals took part in a variety of games including "climbing the greasy pole," obstacle races and "walking a revolving pole." Gibson recalls how he saw hundreds of children ranging from ages six or seven down to toddler size all "burrowing" away in a large heap of sand. The children worked with spoons, cups, shovels, handcarts while some just used their hands. He observed that all the children "looked strong and healthy" and not like the English children who lived in large towns. (4)

Gibson wrote about the diet of the poor of St Petersburg. He stated that they ate a large amount of "sunflower seeds" and a pastry which did not contain much "butter or dripping" and had a filling of either boiled rice or sago. He saw large "8lb or 10lb" black rye bread loaves being sold in the streets and markets. Although the bread did not look very "appetizing" the people appeared to be "hardy and strong." (4)

There was a stark contrast in this vibrant, stunning city between the common folk and nobility. Many of the poorer classes wore "sheepskins" and had "pieces of skin" tied over their feet for shoes. Whereas the gentry frequented fashionable restaurants such as the "Bear" where the waiters spoke French. (French, at the time, was the official language of the Russian court.) Princes and dukes could be found here at meal times decked out in their "splendid" uniforms and "blazing decorations." Special correspondent, Albert Kinross, who visited the "Bear" stated that St Petersburg "society is brilliant" and the ladies wore "such diamonds" that could only be seen "exhibited" or on display at "fashionable jewellers." Furthermore the diamonds seen in St Petersburg were famous because of their size – they "frequently" measured "half an inch" across with a diameter the same. (5)

Kinross was "enchanted" by the men who had made "ravishing toilets." He describes them as "bronzed" and "bearded heroes" in ankle length coats who carried "oriental swords" and "yatagahans" [2] hanging on belts of silver. There were also generals who wore "wide trousers" with knee-high leather boots. All of the men wore resplendent medals and crosses. (5)

In 1902, Augustus I. C. Hare, a travel guide writer, reflected that in the summer months there were not many "aristocratic equipages", on the streets of St Petersburg as "all nobility" were on holiday in the countryside. (6)

The Sanders family lived on the fringes of this nobility. Not only did Tom and his family spend some summer months at family estates they also spent many holidays abroad; their childhood was "crammed with passports, visas and foreign hotels." Ultimately, they visited nearly every country in Europe. (7)

One favourite holiday destination for the aristocracy of St Petersburg in the early twentieth century was Imatra, Finland. Nevertheless, tourists had plenty of choice of destination because all parts of Europe were easily accessible by train or steamer.

The Sanders' and their extended family are thought to have had numerous country estates in Russia, Finland and Estonia. Hollywood columnist, Harrison Carroll mentions that they had a "nine-acre" estate near to Melitopol where battle was ensuing in 1943. Tom had the deeds to the property and hoped one day to regain ownership of it. (8)

[2] A yatagahan is a type of short sabre or Ottoman knife

Melitopol is a city in southern Ukraine near to the Crimea. It was an area where many of Russia's nobility spent the summer months. Notably, the British battleship HMS Marlborough rescued 17 of the Russian Imperial Family from Yalta, Crimea, Ukraine on 11th April 1919. The royal party included Queen Alexandra's sister, the Dowager Empress Marie, (Tsar Nicholas' mother), the tsar's sister the Grand Duchess Xenia and Prince Felix Yusupov who was renowned for being involved with the assassination of Grigori Rasputin. Ladies in waiting, governesses and other servants travelled with them into permanent exile to different countries across the world. (9)

Grand Duchess Xenia's was given grace and favour accommodation by King George V at Wilderness House, Hampton Court, England after her exile. Tom's cousin, Mara Sanders (Dagmar Sophie Sanders), became her assistant and companion in the late 1930's after Xenia's long-time friend and aide, Sophie Evreinoff, died at the age of 65 in 1935. (10)

Mara, whose family is thought to have been involved with the Russian royal family for some years, was born at Peterhof, St Petersburg in 1900. She came to England with her mother, Dagmar (Dinne) Sanders, and her father, George Frederick William Sanders, who had worked as a British diplomat in St. Petersburg. It is not clear how Mara and her family escaped Russia but they returned to London in 1917. (11)

Russo – Japanese War 1904 - 1905

Tsar Nicholas II was a feeble ruler who was opposed to a representative government or duma. Therefore, the defeat by Japan when the two countries clashed over their respective interests in the Far East did nothing to improve his public image.

Poor diplomacy ultimately led to war. In 1904, Japan attacked the Russian naval base of Port Arthur (near Dalian, today's China). Defeat followed on land and sea and the final catastrophe came in May 1905 when the entire Baltic fleet, which had sailed the long way round Africa to relieve Port Arthur, was sunk in the Tsushima Straits off Japan. The British had refused to allow the Russians to use the Suez Canal.

In September 1905, a badly beaten Russia signed the Treaty of Portsmouth (New Hampshire), USA under the terms of which gave up Port Arthur, Dalian and Southern Sakhalin Island as well as any claims to Korea. However, it retained its presence in Manchuria.

1905 Revolution

There was widespread unrest in Russia after the fall of Port Arthur, China. On 9th January 1905 Georgy Apollonovich Gapon, a radical Russian Orthodox priest, led a crowd of about 200,000 workers – men, women and children to the Winter Palace in St Petersburg to petition the tsar for better working conditions. They sang, "God Save the Tsar" but imperial guards opened fire on them killing several hundred. This day would be remembered as 'Bloody Sunday.'

The country broke out into anarchy. There were wild strikes, pogroms, mutinies and killings of landowners and industrialists. In St Petersburg, social democrat activists were forming soviets (workers councils). A general strike was declared which brought the country to a standstill in October 1905.

In essence, at the time of Tom Sanders' birth and the following year Russia and notably St Petersburg was going through a period of great instability and revolutionary unrest as well as being at war with Japan.

The Sanders Family History

Tom (Conway) Sanders, who in later years played many detective roles in the movies, on television and radio, would have had to use all his investigative skills to discover who his father's ancestors really were. His father, Henry Peter Ernest Sanders, was born in St Petersburg on 20th October 1868. Henry declared at his marriage to Margaret Kolbe on 11th December 1903 that his father was Paul Sanders. Henry's occupation was 'Assistant director of rope factory'. (12) It is believed that when Henry Sanders married he was given a position in Hoth Rope Works by his father in law, Robert Kolbe.

Paul Sanders had allegedly been born in London around the middle of the nineteenth century. (13) There is no trace in any of the UK birth, baptism or census records of a Paul Sanders in London in the 1840's. Furthermore, the name Paul Sanders does not feature very often in any UK family history records for the 1800's and those that appear do not have appeared to have any connection with the Sanders' of St Petersburg.

However, a Peter Frederick Ernest Sanders born St Petersburg about 1841 marries Matilda Maria Harvey in London in 1865. His brother, Friedrich Christian Heinrich Sanders born St Petersburg around 1843 married Matilda's sister, Rosalie Albertine Harvey in 1869. Peter and Fredriech's father was Ernest Ludwig Sanders who arrived in London in 1859 as an alien.

Peter F.E. Sanders became a naturalised UK citizen in 1888. He stated he was a Commission Agent, originally from Oldenburg (Grand Duchy) but born in St Petersburg and married but with no children.

In 1943, while living in the United States, during the war years, H.P. Sanders applied for social security citing his father as Paul Sanders and mother Matilda Harvey?

Henry Sanders was a fine balalaika player who formed his own orchestra and prepared the musical arrangements himself. His orchestra became very popular and it was not long before he was playing for the Russian royal family. Apparently, he was decorated so many times by the emperor for merit that he "jingled" as he walked. The balalaika in those days was regarded as a vulgar instrument that was only played by the peasants who lived along the River Volga. (15)

The question of the Sanders' nationality is quite baffling. For example Alan Napier, actor friend of George Sanders, said that George had told him that his father was illegitimate and probably of Russian descent. (16) George Sanders once told a journalist that he was a "quarter" Russian because his mother was half Russian. (7) Tom's sister, Margaret Sanders Bloecker, wrote to actor Brian Aherne after George's death and told him that she and her brothers had not been told the truth by their parents concerning their father's pedigree. They had been told that he was orphaned as a young child. She had discovered from a relative, believed to be the aforementioned Dagmar Sophie Sanders (Mara), that her father was allegedly the illegitimate son of a Russian countess and a Prince of Oldenburg who was married to one of the tsar's sisters. She relayed the same information to Richard Vanderbeets, the author of *An Exhausted Life*. (13) (17)

Tsar Alexander III was on the throne of Russia in 1868, the year of Henry Sanders birth. He had two sisters; Grand Duchess Alexandra Alexandrovna of Russia (1842-1949) and Grand Duchess Maria Alexandrovna (1853-1920). Grand Duchess Marie married Prince Albert, Duke of Edinburgh, the second son of Queen Victoria.

Yet, some Dukes of Oldenburg did marry into the Russian royal family notably Duke George of Oldenburg (1784 – 1812). He married Grand Duchess Catherine Pavlovna of Russia, daughter of Paul 1 of Russia. Then in 1901 Tsar Nicholas II's sister Grand Duchess Olga Alexandrovna married Duke Peter Alexandrovich of Oldenburg (1868 – 1924). Neither of the two above mentioned Dukes of Oldenburg could have been the father of Henry Sanders, the former having died years before Henry's birth and the latter being born the same year as Henry.

However, from what Alan Napier allegedly said along with George Sanders remarks in his autobiography *Memoirs of a Professional Cad* about his father arriving with the "mail" it all dubiously points to the fact that George knew about his father's illegitimacy. On the other hand, he may have been making an educated guess because he did not really believe what he had been told by his father. (18) Questionably Tom also knew something about his father's antecedents or lack of because he declared his nationality as "Scotch/British" (his mother's ancestry) on a Mexican border crossing card in 1940. (19)

Like all families there were bound to be a number of skeletons in the Sanders' closet. For example in some 1953 newspapers there were reports concerning the reason why George Sanders was near to cracking up emotionally at that time. It claims that he was worried about an elder brother who was in prison in Hungary, clarifying that it was not his older brother, Tom Conway. (20) It was in fact Edgar Sanders, his cousin, brother of Mara Sanders. What is also surprising is that in the book, *Once a Grand Duchess*, Mara is referred to as George Sanders' sister. (10) Could Tom's father, Henry Sanders also have been the father of Edgar and Mara Sanders? Or were both reports, albeit years apart, wrong?

Brian Aherne was also puzzled by an Italian countess of Russian decent who he met when he and his wife went to dinner with George

Sanders and his third wife, Benita Hume in Rome. Benita told Brian that the lady was George's "half-sister" but not to say anything about it. (17)

Unfortunately, whilst oral history can be an extremely valuable source of information for the genealogist, without documentary proof to back up Henry Sanders' alleged connection with royalty, the story has to remain a very interesting family story only at this time. Perhaps some of the relevant documentation may have been among the papers that George Sanders allegedly burnt prior to his death.

On the other hand Tom's mother, Margaret Bertha Jenney Kolbe Sanders', ancestry is much easier to trace. She was born in St Petersburg in about 1884 to Robert Wilhelm Kolbe and Marie or Mary Hoth. Margaret or Margarethe was baptised on 9th May 1884 at St Catharina I Church, St Petersburg, believed to be a Lutheran Church. (21)

Mary Hoth was the daughter of Wilhelm Hoth, a businessman and granddaughter of John Hoth (stockbroker), believed founder of Hoth Rope Works on the River Neva, St Petersburg. John Hoth had been born in St Petersburg

Hoth Rope Works is thought to have been established in St Petersburg in the early nineteenth century. An exact date has not been established. However, for example, in July 1834 a crank type engine was ordered by Baring Brothers & Co for "Rope Works in St Petersburg on the River Neva side." It was a 30 hp engine with a cylinder disc size of 29" x 5' and ran at 21 ½ a second. The owner of the engine was to be J Hoth. (22)

In September 1900 it was reported by *The Hocking Sentinal* that the "Hoth English rope works of St Petersburg" was burnt down with a loss of $750,000. (23) It is not clear if this was deliberate act or an accident. There were a great many reports over the years of fires in St Petersburg. Twelve years later, another fire, which started in a timber yard on Petrovsky Ostrov, completely destroyed the Palace of Peter the Great. (24)

Margaret Kolbe Sanders' paternal grandfather was Ernst Ludwig Kolbe, a St Petersburg businessman, who along with other entrepreneurs founded the Narva Krenholm Cotton Products Mill PLC in Estonia in 1857. The business was located on the Narva River near to the Narva Falls. (25)

Margaret Kolbe Sanders could trace her British ancestry back to seventeenth century Dundee, Scotland where her ancestor Thomas Clayhills was born the son of a merchant in 1626. (13) He migrated to Danzig (Gdansk) in around 1639 and then later to Riga, Latvia. He had three sons, Johann, Thomas and Hermann Clayhills who subsequently relocated to Tallinn, Estonia.

Johann Clayhills became mayor of Tallinn in 1684 and married the daughter of businessman, Thomas von Drenteln. The daughter inherited the family business, established around 1633, and they renamed it Thomas Clayhills & Sons. In 1679, Tallinn's trading post, Thomas Clayhills & Sons, was established and it became an important force in Tallinn and a part of its history. (26)

In the late 18th century, Thomas Clayhills & Sons bought its first ships. It imported mostly salt, iron, herring, cod, tobacco and hops. It first exported flax, grain and timber, then later asbestos and cement. It developed contracts with Germany, Denmark, England and Russia. It is believed that Thomas Clayhills & Sons was the oldest trading company in Estonia and one of the oldest in Europe. (27)

Johann Clayhills bought a house on Pikk 13, Tallinn in 1729 and opened one of the first merchant stores there. Today the building is a gastro pub called 'CLAYHILLS'. The medieval part of Tallinn, with its narrow twisting cobbled streets and fairy-tale turrets, has been preserved and there are plenty of places to eat and visit. [3]

Jonas Hanaway, an eighteenth century merchant on his travels, visited Tallinn for one day and wrote that "Mr Thomas Clayhills, a considerable person in this place, and the only English merchant, entertained me with great hospitality and politeness." (28)

It is clear then that Tom Sanders was born into a very affluent and high-ranking society with an impressive maternal ancestry. In the early 20th century, there were about 80,000 nobles, by birth and 150,000 who held noble rank due to their contribution to society living in St Petersburg.

As a young boy growing up, Tom would have been afforded all the privileges that a wealthy family could provide. However he recalled that if he had "a horse," or a "boat" his brother had to have the same. His parents "played no favourites" and the boys shared

---

[3] Author visited Tallinn in 2013 and 2014

everything. The Sanders children were also taught "discipline, honesty and loyalty". (29)

Henry and Margaret Sanders belonged to the Anglo-Russian expatriate business community, which was centred in St Petersburg from the 1730s to the 1920's. Some families had been living in Russia for many generations but usually retained their British citizenship and sent their children to school in England. Unsurprisingly, some Brits had lived in Russia for so long their English accents acquired a distinctive intonation peculiar to Anglo-Russians.

Henry Sanders had a very unusual English accent. He can be heard briefly in *Appointment in London* (1943) in which he plays a cameo role as George Sanders' father. Tom's cousin, Edgar Adolph Sanders, however, spoke English with a hint of a Russian intonation. Edgar Sanders can be seen on film shot by British Pathe News in 1953 at Croydon Airport, England giving an interview. He had just been released from a Hungarian prison for alleged spying. This was an international news event at the time. Edgar Sanders was a quietly spoken, handsome man of 6' 3" who bore more than a passing resemblance to George Sanders. (30)

There would have come a time when the Sanders' had to make the decision about their eldest son's future education and as there was less than two years between Tom and George they no doubt thought it best to send the boys away together so that they had each other for company. Therefore with money no object, it was decided that the Sanders boys would attend good boarding schools in England with the intention of turning them into "brilliant examples of English youth." (29)

It is not clear if the boys would have definitely been educated in England had it not been for the outbreak of World War I. Likewise the ongoing problems of civil unrest in St Petersburg may have assisted the Sanders' in making their final decision.

Fig 3: Cruiser AURORA.   St Petersburg, Russia 2014

Photograph by C.E.Parkinson ©

The Russian Revolution began when at 0945hrs on 25 October 1917 a blank shot from Aurora's forecastle gun signalled the start of the assault on the Winter Palace, St Petersburg.

"Stick up your hands!"
England
1915 - 1923

Tom Sanders began his formal education in England at Dunhurst Preparatory School, Hampshire, in the autumn of 1915 aged 11 years. (31) He had travelled to England with his mother, brother and sister. No doubt, the Sanders' journey to England would have been a perilous one with the Germans patrolling the Baltic and North Sea. The German fleet could pass easily into the Baltic via the Kiel Canal without being observed.

Some sources state the Sanders children were privately educated at home until 1915. (13) However, the H.W.Wilson Co. *Year Book* notes that George Sanders began his education at a Russian school. (32) Similarly George recalled in an interview that he had attended Russian "grammar schools." (7) One would assume that Tom also attended the same schools but it has not been possible to confirm or deny this.

Arguably both accounts might be true. It is possible that the Sanders children were educated in school in term times and privately educated at home during the summer months. On the other hand they may have began by attending some of St Petersburgs schools but may have been taken out by their parents like the American Ambassador to Russia, Charlemayne Tower, did. He discovered that his three children's "command" of other languages like French and German were far better than their English. Ultimately he sent his children back to the United States to be educated. (33)

Tom's mother took up residence in England to settle the boys into school. She remained there because Henry Sanders had seen suspicious activity in St Petersburg and suspected there was going to be trouble. (15)

However, in 1916, Margaret received a letter from her husband telling her that there was no fear of revolution in Russia so it was all right for her to return. Margaret Sanders indeed returned to St Petersburg in the summer of 1916 taking young Margaret with her. Tom and George remained in England. (18)

Yet, it was not long after Margaret's arrival in St Petersburg that things there worsened. Therefore, Henry and Margaret Sanders, with their daughter, fled to Finland and spent the winter there. Margaret Sanders and her daughter, Margaret, eventually travelled back to England in 1917. Henry must have returned to St Petersburg at some point because later in 1917 he escaped in haste, fearing for his life across the frozen ice fields to Finland believed on a horse drawn sledge. (18) (34) (15)

George Sanders wrote in his autobiography, *Memoirs of a Professional Cad*, that as he was leaving St Petersburg on one train, Lenin was arriving on another. The scene he describes at the station where he is waved off by his father, affluent friends and relatives is no doubt true but in fact, the date was either 1914 or 1915 when he and Tom left St Petersburg for the last time. (18) Lenin arrived back in Petrograd (St Petersburg) in a sealed train on 3rd April 1917. In 1914 Lenin, who had been living in Poland, moved to Switzerland. (35)

Nevertheless, both of the Sanders brother's Hollywood scripted biographies centre on the fact that they fled Russia at the time of revolution in 1917. Tom said that he succeeded in fleeing from Russia when he was "barely 13." (36) It all sounds very dramatic but he was most probably sticking to the wording of the bios. It is true that he would have been 13 in 1917 but both he and George had been at school in England at the time and there is no suggestion that either boy returned to Russia after 1915.

Unhappily, many of Tom's relatives and family friends did not escape the Bolsheviks and were imprisoned or murdered. (18) It is believed that between 900,000 and 2 million white émigré escaped from Russia between 1917 and 1920, among them were people from all walks of life and ethnic groups; intellectuals of various professions, dispossessed businessmen, landowners, imperial politicians, Cossacks and soldiers.

Journalist, Hamilton Fife, had reported that all the time he was in Russia he noticed that the "kettle" of revolution was "getting hotter." He went on to say that it was not until the spring of 1915 that it's "singing" could be heard in the "open." (37) Some people had the foresight to leave St Petersburg which leads one to wonder why so many ex-pats stayed there so long.

Tom moved up to Bedales School in the autumn of 1917. (31) He believed the decision to send him to this "famous" school was possibly one of the "gravest mistakes" his parents had ever made because he never intended to do any worthwhile study there. His "educational enlightenment" he described as no more than a "series of escapades" and the money his parents spent on his education was totally wasted. From the outset he endeavoured to spend his time at Bedales being as disruptive as possible. (29)

Tom recalled that he and George were "fiendish" "brats", adding that when they were not "actually in trouble" they were conspiring how to get into trouble or to get others into trouble. They got on very well together and rarely fell out with each other because they had the same "disinterest" in anything "constructive or respectable". (29)

At one time Tom, along with George and a number of other students hatched a plan to run away from school. Tom tells how they were going to live in the woods on a fellow escapees family estate, sixty miles away, until the holidays. The boys did manage to escape from school but were soon found by a "bulky matron" on a motorcycle who herded them back where Tom and George were given a "terrific hiding" by the school officials, then by their parents. (29)

Beneath his quiet facade Tom possessed a devious streak combined with a cheeky sense of humour which he used time and again throughout his life. He was never afraid of getting in trouble and enjoyed the thrill of making trouble in his quiet unassuming manner.

Tom was unsettled, unhappy, and longed to be in Mustamakki, Finland once more where he had spent many carefree times even though he appears to have enjoyed the leafy, Hampshire countryside. Both he and his brother were being bullied by other pupils at the school so this was probably why they tried so hard to get other people into trouble to mask their own insecurities. (13)

It appears that Margaret Sanders did not write to Tom very often and her visits to see her children were infrequent. Arguably Tom's bad behaviour could be blamed on the fact that he lacked the loving family attention that he had experienced at home in St Petersburg. The only way he could attract his parents attention was to be as disruptive as possible. Perhaps this could have been the root of personal insecurities which would hound him for the rest of his life.

Bedales is a liberal, co-ed school located in Steep, Hampshire, England. It is still one of the most expensive public schools in England with the fees comparable to Harrow and Eton. The curriculum in Tom's day would have provided a good grounding in English and modern languages, science, design, drama, carpentry, gardening and nature study. This was probably where he learnt his carpentry skills and where his love of designing boats, aeroplanes and inventing stems from.

Tom's education did not get any better even after frequent chastisement by the prefects. Eventually he got so sick of continually being reprimanded he decided to put a stop to it. He knew that one of his fellow students had a pistol so he says he manged to persuade this person to sell it to him. Knowing Tom he probably put pressure on him to part with it or may even have stolen it. The next time he attended the prefects office for punishment he was told he was in trouble again but Tom had other ideas. He pulled out the gun and said: "stick up your hands!" (29)

The following day his parents were summoned to the school to speak with the school head. The outcome of the interview resulted in Tom being expelled. As previously mentioned this disruptive behaviour employed by him was the only way he could get his parents attention, which he ultimately did. Here was a teenage boy, who had been uprooted from his privileged, calm and happy upbringing, and sent to an alien country. A boy who had little or no contact with his mother whom he clearly adored, being bullied by other pupils and was having to come to terms with the loss of his birthright. He was also having to live with the knowledge that he was not going to return to his affluent old life in Russia any time soon. (29)

Enquiries have been made, via email, with the archivist at Bedales School and unfortunately there is no "headmaster's correspondence" or any records from that "era that would shed any light on the matter" of Tom's expulsion. However, both Tom and George are recorded leaving Bedales in July 1919. Bedales have records of minutes of staff meetings but they were quite mundane and only mention the need for the students to be more punctual when going to class. The archivist checked the school's address list for 1933 and it still showed Tom's father's address as Petroffsky Ostroff 6, Petrograd – she added that she did not believe that the information had not been updated since he was at school. (31)

George Sanders mentions his brother's expulsion in *Memoirs of a Professional Cad* and is not pleased because his parents decided he would have to leave the school as well. This is the only reference to his brother in his biography which serves to highlight the fact that he and Tom had probably become estranged by the time it was written in 1960. George's version of the story claims that Tom pulled the gun out on a teacher who was telling him to get to class as he was late. (18)

Henry and Margaret Sanders decided to send Tom and George to Brighton College, Sussex. The college was renowned for its "firmness" and Tom was "caned" often. He was taught how to behave but learned very little else. (29) Years later he admitted that he had had a lukewarm ambition to be an engineer in his early years. Nevertheless he only had one aim in college and that was to get through it as easily and swiftly as possible. (38)

By this time the Sanders family had lost their considerable fortune and had to rely on Margaret Sanders relatives to assist them monetarily. Brighton College was not as prestigious as some of the other private schools in England. On reflection it must have been very hard for the boys to adjust to the fact that their family had fallen on hard times and they could not have everything that they wanted.

Tom appeared to have enjoyed boxing at college as he became heavy-weight champion while he was there. (39) He also became an accomplished swimmer. He was no doubt coached by Sergeant Major S.J. Beckett (Sarge) who joined the staff of Brighton College in 1919. "Sarge" taught boxing, swimming, gymnastics and physical training lessons. In the April 1920 edition of the *Brighton College Magazine* there is a report of how boxing had improved since his appointment. (40)

Communcation has been made with the archivist at Brighton College but there does not appear to be any information relating to Tom's time there. They confirm he attended the school between 1919 – 1922 and he was a member of Dunford House.

In 1922 Tom, age 17, left Brighton College having only been there for three years. After graduation he opted to go to South Africa to earn a living.

"I had plenty of rope"
South Africa
1923 - 1929

There is a short gap in Tom's history between the Summer of 1922 when he left Brighton College and 23rd June 1923 when he emigrated to make his fortune in South Africa. Obtaining and filling out the necessary forms and the like for the Colonial Office would have undoubtedly been time consuming in itself. Tom was living at 21 Wordsworth Road, Worthing, West Sussex at the time that he sailed since this address is cited on the ship's manifest. (45)

His father, Henry Sanders, would later name the address above as to where he went into receivership in 1934. The initial petition for liquidation was filed on 26th July 1934. (41) The application for discharge of bankruptcy hearing was dated July 18th 1935 at Brighton, Sussex. (42) Ironically his son, George Sanders, would also go bankrupt thirty years later following the collapse of his Cadco company.

The impression given by Vanderbeets in *An Exhausted Life* is that Tom went to Rhodesia in 1921 to work in a cotton mill and returned to England eight years later in 1929. (13) Brighton College's *Old Brightonians* website notes that Tom attended the college between 1919 – 1922. Tom himself stated that he went to Rhodesia when he was 18 years old. He would not have been eighteen until September 1922 and there is no trace of him sailing to South Africa before 1923. There is no mention in any records located so far that Tom worked in a cotton mill. Likewise he never mentioned that fact in any of his interviews. It is not inconceivable but in 1921 the cotton industry had not taken off in Rhodesia and cotton growing was still in the "experimental stage" in 1922. (43)

In a bid to accelerate the rate of emigration of its people to the Empire, the British the Empire Settlement Act of 1922 which stated that the British government would assist the migration of suitable people government called a meeting of representatives from Canada, Australia and New Zealand to consult on the viability of initiating a large scale policy of state-aided settlement within the Empire. The consultative meeting formed the basis for who intended to settle in any part of the Empire. Assistance schemes were to be of two types: development or land settlement or assisting settlement through providing help in the form of passages, initial allowances, training etcetera. The British Government contributed financially to the settlement scheme with the understanding that its contribution would not exceed half the expenses of any scheme. As a direct result of this scheme Rhodesia received some 300 settlers in the next three years, one of them being Thomas C Sanders. (43)

South Africa was going through a period of political change in the early 1920's. In 1923 the country was split up into different territories. It had previously been governed by the British South African Company but the colonists wanted local rule. It was subsequently divided up into North Rhodesia and South Rhodesia. The British wanted to recruit as many white immigrants as possible as they were keen to form a British colony there. That could have been one of the reasons why there was a delay in Tom emigrating – he was waiting or had to wait for the territories to be established.

In making his decision to go to Rhodesia Tom may have read an article similar to the one featured in the *Western Mercury Star* advertising the benefits of African cattle ranching. It boasted that a "rancher leads a free independent, open air life" with the potential to make "good livings". (44) What more could a young man with an adventurous mind and a yearning for the quiet wide open spaces want? Tom admitted that he had an adventurous spirit as he had spent his spare time at Bedales reading "hair – raising stories". He would go on to describe himself years later as being a "rugged" character at this time. (29)

Tom sails to South Africa

Tom sailed to Port Natal (Durban) South Africa on 23rd June 1923 from London on board the SS Umtali, owned by Bullard and King Co. Ltd, London. The Umtali was built in 1896 in Sunderland, England, by James Laing. It was later sold in 1925 to Yugoslavia and renamed SOLUN. The ships manifest shows that Tom was aged 18, his occupation 'Cattle Rancher' and in the 'Country of Permanent Residence' column it reads 'Rhodesia'. (45) This is proof that Tom had emigrated and had intended to make Rhodesia his domicile.

Although this was probably a great adventure at the time no doubt Tom would have arrived in Durban with a sense of trepidation mixed with excitement. Arguably he was a seasoned traveller having travelled extensively to different parts of Europe as a child combined with being used to living away from home when at school.

It is not clear what form Tom's occupation as a cattle rancher took. It is possible he had assistance with his passage to South Africa and once in Rhodesia he probably attended training in animal husbandry and ranching; this training may have lasted a few months. It is logical to believe that during his training Tom decided that this job was not for him and concluded that more money could be made quicker elsewhere. On the other hand he may not have taken up cattle ranching straight away and been tempted to work elsewhere, perhaps in mining. Gold for example was valued at £2,998 for 569oz in Rhodesia in 1920 which works out at £102,606.87 today. (43)

Tom appears to have been a very independent person, and a dreamer who liked the wide open spaces. He was a young man seeking his fortune hoping to make something of himself without the help of his parents. However his initial rush of eagerness did not last long. He would admit nearly twenty years later that he was "enthusiastic" to new ideas and conceptions but was not the "perservering type." (29) This was a correct self-assessment as Tom never stayed in one job for very long.

Life in Northern Rhodesia would have been very hard for the pioneer and the chance of making a lot of money in ranching or any other occupation would have been very difficult in the early years.

The weather, in Northern Rhodesia, is tropical with a dry and rainy season. The Colonial Report for Northern Rhodesia 1924 – 25 states that normally the rainy season starts in November and usually ends in April with very few rainy days after that. (46)

Tom had arrived in Rhodesia during one of the driest years for years. In fact the season 1923 – 1924 was "remarkable" for the "scarcity" of rain whereas 1924 – 25 was exceptionally wet throughout the whole country. Rainfall recorded at Livingstone between October 1924 and April 1925 was 54 inches whereas it would normally be 30 inches. Mean maximum temperatures for Livingstone were 93.5 degrees Farenheit for any one month with the lowest being in July 61.5 degrees. (46)

The white population of the country was very small and there were probably not many people of Tom's age. There had not been an official census carried out in Northern Rhodesia but on 1st April 1924 there were 4,182 Europeans in the country, 1,919 adult males and 1,016 adult females. There were 107 births recorded and 40 deaths. (46)

A point of interest is that in 1920, founder of Rhodesia, Cecil Rhodes', body was transferred to a grave on Malindizimu Hill or Worlds View, a granite hill about 40 km south of Bulawayo. Towards the end of his stay in South Africa Tom worked as a guide driving tourists to see Rhodes tomb. (36) It is therefore safe to assume that he was living in Bulawayo, Southern Rhodesia for a time. A road ran from Bulawayo to World's View and consequently numerous Bulawayon hotels and car companies "thrived" by taking advantage of the tourists wanting to make a trip to the site. (47)

Tom indicated that he spent his time in South Africa undertaking labouring in gold, asbestos and copper mines. He later became an assistant superintendant in an asbestos mine. (38) The main asbestos mining area being near Bulawayo. Tom learnt the native languages, made friends with "rebellious blacks" went "broke" and nearly died from the "effects of the malaria" that prompted him to return home prematurely. (29) Ultimately Tom who was ailing, and having no funds, borrowed the fare home and left South Africa for good.

It was not unusual for immigrants to find themselves destitute in South Africa at this time. For example in 1931 one hundred and fifty one indigent people were repatriated to other regions or overseas at the expense of the government. (48)

When interviewed years later Tom remarked that he nearly starved when he worked in a gold mine. Apparently the wages were good but he gambled his money away playing cards. This leads one to suspect that he had been gambling to try to make enough money to either leave the country or make his fortune more quickly. One can only try imagine what the conditions were like working in a mine in South Africa at this time. (36)

On 2nd Nov 1929 Tom arrived back in London having returned from Rhodesia via Cape Town, South Africa on board the SS Trafford Hall, official number 120906. It would have been at least a seventeen day voyage which means he would have left South Africa near the middle of October 1929. (49)

SS Trafford Hall was owned by Hall Line Limited and at the time was a cargo passenger ship built in Glasgow in 1905. The ship was scrapped in the 1930's. Tom was travelling in First Class and his occupation was "sampler". Considering he had been working in gold, copper, and asbestos mines suggests he may have been, at one time, in charge of looking for the best seams of minerals. He gave his home address as Sussex Cottage, Feltham Park, Leatherhead, Surrey; his family's home. (49)

Consequently Tom returned to England while he was still able to do so. His father, Henry Sanders, believed that if a man was given "enough rope he'd hang himself". Tom told reporter Ernest Foster that he personally had "plenty of rope" which stretched "all the way from Russia to England to South Africa and then the long way from there to Hollywood." (36)

"I was a good type"
England
1929 - 1939

Tom recalled that when he finally returned to "Liverpool" he called George who was in London and told him where he was and explained that he was staying in a hotel until he could solve the problem of getting "transportation home." George allegedly turned up at the hotel in the middle of the night and surprised Tom. This suggests that Tom had no money, because there was a perfectly good train service from Liverpool to London. However, this remark in itself was odd because Tom disembarked, according to the ships manifest, in London on 2nd November 1929. (29) (49)

It was over a month later that George arrived back from South America disembarking at Liverpool on 28th December 1929. There are a number of possibly explanations of the account that Tom gave to *Screenland Magazine*. 1) Embellished story by Conway or the magazine to make the story sound more exciting or plausible. 2) Tom did indeed go to Liverpool instead of going straight home. 3) He went to Liverpool to meet George but missed him.

Reading between the lines it would appear that Tom was probably short of funds and contacted George to bail him out. He had been out of the country for six years so one would have surmised that he would have wanted to go straight home. Why would he wait for a month or more before going home? Unless he was too embarrassed to go home because he was broke or did not want his family to see the condition he was in. Similarly, why go to Liverpool which was much further away from home than London and if he had no money how did he get there? In all probability he was staying in London without funds and not wanting to burden his family contacted George who was probably at home in Surrey.

Nevertheless, on returning to England Tom spent time convalescing from malaria because he had been so ill and as a consequence he was now extremely thin. He was once the older and bigger brother but now he found that George was taller than him by two inches. When feeling better he was eager to find a job as soon as possible. This was not a good time in England to look for a job because unemployment was around the three million mark nationally at the beginning of the 1930's.

Tom was one of the fortunate ones because he had a number of jobs between 1930 – 1939, from running a yacht yard in the south of England (believed to be owned by his parents), working as an engineer in a carburettor factory, selling safety glass for a safety glass company, and acting on stage and radio. He used his family home in Surrey as his base for most of the time he was working in England. His name can be found on the electoral roll for Epsom, Surrey between 1930 and 1935 inclusive. However, he does not appear on that roll between 1936 and 1938. At that time, he would have been touring as a stage actor. In 1939, his name can be once more found in the Surrey electoral rolls. (50)

In the early 1930's Tom and George were given singing lessons by their Uncle Sasha. Sasha came to England after the Russian Revolution and according to actress Anna Lee, he was now working as an interpreter and singing teacher. (Other sources suggest that only George received the singing lessons (17) (13)) Sasha visited Anna Lee every week to give her lessons and on one occasion, he took Tom and George with him. (51) Brian Aherne mentions in *A Dreadful Man* that Sasha was an alcoholic, "professional houseguest" who was a favourite with the Sanders boys. (17)

Around the middle of the 1930's Tom got a job as a salesman for a safety glass manufacturer. One day a man came in to the store and was more interested in Tom as an ideal candidate for a part he was casting in a production for a Little Theatre Company in London than buying glass. Tom made a bargain with him; he would do the play if the man put in a large order for glass. (38)

That was how Tom drifted into acting. His first play was *No 17* written by British author, Jefferson J. Farjeon. The play was such a success that Tom was approached by the head of a repertory company who offered him work, he accepted and ended up touring with several companies around the country for a year and a half.

"Sometimes one has no idea he can act," said Tom but a Little Theatre Company will "bring it out of him if it is there." Tom had found his true vocation and he liked it. During his English stage career, he appeared in between twenty-five and thirty plays such as *Dangerous Corner, Private Lives,* and *By Candlelight.* (52)

An article in *The South Manchester Reporter* concerning the Manchester Athenaeum Drama Society, states that Tom Conway was a former member of their company and he was possibly the most renowned. In 2010, the Manchester Athenaeum Drama Society proclaimed to be the oldest amateur dramatic group in the world. (53)

In the 1930's Tom made numerous radio broadcasts for the British Broadcasting Company (BBC). In 1922, the general manager of the BBC, Lord Reith, adopted 'Received Pronunciation' as the broadcasting standard for broadcasters. Therefore, Tom would have received voice-coaching lessons to bring him up to the required standard. His brother George also worked for the BBC therefore is it any wonder that their voices sounded similar. Incidentally there were no regional British accents heard on radio until the Second World War.

It was at his brother, George's, insistence that Tom joined him in Hollywood where he was already making a name for himself as an actor. George wrote to his father giving him a multitude of tips and instructions as to how Tom should go about getting into British films first before venturing across the Atlantic. Further information about this can be found in *An Exhausted Life* (Vanderbeets) (13) and *A Dreadful Man* (Aherne). (17)

Tom was not successful in getting into British films. He had taken a screen test in London in 1937 believed to have been organised by George and was told that he did not "photograph well". (17) A couple of years later Tom said that England was in "the doldrums" and the acting work had "fallen off." At this time, the country was preparing for the possibility of war and everything was up in the air. (29)

George Sanders started making long distance calls trying to encourage Tom to join him. Eventually when he told Tom that he had purchased a yacht that made up Tom's mind and he set out for Hollywood. Tom says that he was feeling "particularly low." (29) It is believed that around this time he may have been working for the family "yacht building" business. (54)

One reason for his apparent feelings of moroseness could have been the fact that the weather in southern England in the early summer of 1939 was terrible with a lot of heavy rain and some really dull days.

A pattern seems to be emerging here. Did Tom suffer from depression when things were not going particularly well? Perhaps he continually thought about the lost family business and fortune in Russia. On the other hand, was he the sort of person who soon tired of a job and had to find something new to enthuse himself? It sounds as if his initial enthusiasm for acting had waned – did he really want to start again?

There is no indication that Tom was envious of his brother at this time nevertheless those feelings could already have been festering in his mind. He had been trying to get into pictures where he believed good money could be made but had no luck. George was beginning to become more successful yet not as much as he would do in the coming years. Tom thought hard and long before deciding to leave England as he had serious reservations, thinking it was not really the right thing to do. After all war was looming, he would be leaving his aging parents behind at a time of uncertainty. On the other hand could Tom's misgivings have had to with the fact that he might not be successful in getting into films in Hollywood?

One point to mention is that Tom would not have been eligible for Military Service in 1939. On 27th April 1939, a limited form of conscription was introduced in the United Kingdom with only single men between aged between 20 and 22 called up. They were called 'militiamen', which served to distinguish them from the regular army. The men were to receive six months training and then be discharged into an active reserve. After which they would be recalled for training periodically and attend an annual camp.

However when war broke out on 3rd September 1939 The National Service Act came into force and those militiamen already conscripted found themselves absorbed into the army. The British government declared in October 1939 that all men between 18 and 41 who were not working in "reserved occupations" were liable to be called up if required. That month men aged between 20 and 23 were required to register and select which armed force they wanted to serve in. As the war progressed, other age groups were "called up".

Hollywood
1939 – 1942

The MGM Years

Tom arrived in San Pedro, California on the MV Amerika on 6th September 1939, having left Southampton, England on 14th August 1939. By the time he arrived in America, Britain and France had already declared war on Germany. (55)

He travelled First Class, under the name on his British passport, Thomas Charles Sanders, siting his brother's address, 1221 North Horn Avenue, Hollywood. According to the ship's manifest, he had $1,000 dollars on him, his nationality was English and his occupation was a "company director". He was aged 34, six foot one with dark hair, dark eyes and dark complexion. No doubt, he had obtained a tan while lounging on deck as he sailed across the Atlantic. On the day he left England the weather turned and became very hot and sunny. (55)

MV Amerika was a cargo/passenger ship owned by the East Asiatic Company and could carry 70 passengers. The shipping route was Copenhagen, Southampton, St Thomas, Panama Canal, Cristobal, Los Angeles, San Francisco, Seattle, and Vancouver.

In 1943, MV Amerika was commandeered by the British, transferred to the Ministry of War Transport, and operated by the United Baltic Corporation. It was torpedoed and sunk by U-306 off Greenland while in convoy HX-234 from Halifax to Liverpool. (56)

Initially Tom went to live with George when he arrived in Hollywood. George led a solitary life but got on well with Tom who, in the early days, was his closest friend. (57) It was not long after his arrival that he was given a screen test and subsequently he successfully signed a contract with MGM initially for a year.

In the 1940 US Federal Census, taken between 13th and 15th April, Tom was still living with George. They had now moved to 1217 Horn Road, Hollywood. This is a very good primary source because it confirms that Tom is now an actor in "Motion Pictures", he is single, and his wages for the 30 weeks prior to the census were $1500. This is proof that he had signed with MGM prior to the census. He is registered under his former name, Thomas Charles Sanders; alien, stating he had lived in London in 1935. Another person living at the same address was Elsie Sanders shown as sister-in-law to the head of the household and her marital status is 'D' (divorced). [4] The head of the household was George Sanders. (58)

However, even though he was receiving his stock salary Tom was not making many films. He went to Mexico for a short visit in March 1940 alone. He returned to San Ysidro, a district of San Diego on the USA/Mexico border, on 3rd March 1940. He told immigration he was an actor working for MGM for a year. (18)

It was reported in the *Fresno Bee* dated 7th May 1940 that Tom had been signed by director, Mervyn Leroy, to play in the film *Escape* (1940) but his name does not appear in the credits. (59) It may of course have been one of the films he appeared in where he was uncredited.

Tom's debut at MGM is believed to have been as the narrator/radio broadcaster of *Waterloo Bridge*, filmed from late January to early February 1940, starring Robert Taylor and Vivien Leigh. He was uncredited; however this is a fine example of the crisp, English-accented orator. Leigh's character, Myra, turns to prostitution to make ends meet and it is understood that it is Tom's voice that you hear as Myra's first client.

The Great Meddler (1940) was a "short" produced by Fred Zinnemann. "Shorts" were made by directors to show off their abilities to film studios. On occasions these were subsequently made into feature films. In this reel Tom played Henry Bergh, founder of the American Society for the Prevention of Cruelty to Animals. Bergh had been appointed secretary and vice consul to the American litigation in St Petersburg, Russia. However, the climate did not agree with him so he quit and began an extensive tour of Europe.

In *The Great Meddler* Burgh is returning from Russia in 1884. He (Conway) is riding in a carriage with his friend, Elbridge Gerry (organiser for the Prevention of Cruelty to Children). Bergh witnesses a coachman hitting his horse and becomes involved in a scuffle. He ascertains that there are no laws to stop the man from beating his horse so prepares an animal protection bill, which quickly becomes law. (60)

---

[4] George Sanders married his first wife Elsie Poole aka Susan Larson on 27th October 1940.

The film ran for about 11 minutes. It was first shown in Australia in September 1940 and advertised there as a "miniature". (61) One of the first reviews of the film in America has been located in *The Motion Picture Daily* dated 30th December 1940. *The Film Daily* review in January 1941 advertised it as 'A Fine Short Subject'. (60) The film was shown extensively in cinemas at the time and was invariably marketed as 'Very Good'.

For some time Tom and George had been urging their parents to come to America by sending countless telegrams and letters. Eventually the old folks gave in and sailed across the Atlantic. (62) They arrived in Quebec, Canada on 29th July 1940 on the Duchess of Bedford. On August 20th 1940, they are shown arriving at Port Huron, Michigan. They cited George Sanders address of 1245 North Doheny Drive, Beverley Hills, California on the manifest. Henry Sanders is 5' 10" and had blue eyes. Margaret Sanders is 5' 7" with brown eyes. The Sanders' stayed in the USA until 1946. (63)

All of the Sanders family lived together in George's "early Spanish, late Sears-Roebuck" mansion in Beverly Hills for a while. Eventually the closeness of his family got too much for George and he moved to an apartment in the Hollywood hills taking Tom and his wife with him. Henry and Margaret Sanders were housed at George's Laguna Beach house. (64)

Tom was given his first credited, supporting role, at MGM in the third and last of the Nick Carter series, *Sky Murder* (1940), starring Walter Pidgeon. In it, he plays the lecherous, Fifth Columnist, Andrew Hendon, who is murdered on a plane. This is the first instance we have of seeing him as he speaks with a near perfect, Oxford English, accent. In later years, he would speak in a more Americanized way to try to distinguish himself from his brother. Film production began on 24th July 1940 and the film was released on 27th September 1940.

The coin toss

Early in his Hollywood career, Tom discovered one of the drawbacks of having a close relative already established in films. He and George were due to appear in a "dramatic radio sketch" which would have been their first appearance together. However, after just "one rehearsal" their plans were "dashed." Apparently the sound technician told Tom that he and George would have to "toss a coin" to decide who was to be in the show because their voices sounded so "identical" that the radio audience would think they were listening to a monologue. (62)

This was not the first time that the Sanders brothers had tossed a coin. In an interview that Tom gave to *Hollywood Magazine* in 1943 he explained how he changed his name to Conway in 1937. (38) The "similarity" of the brother's voices and "manner" of speaking proved very confusing and they often got each others phone calls during the time they were both working in England. (29) George on the other hand had apparently told Tom he did not want him using his surname when he went to Hollywood. Tom told Frances Dee, on the set of *I Walked With a Zombie*, that when he lost the coin toss he put the coin into a "payphone" and dialled a random set of numbers. "Conways Fish Market" (65) announced the person at the other end and that was how he got his name.

A number of articles have suggested that Tom did not mind his name being changed but debatably that was not always the case. It was partially correct as he did not worry about it all the time he was doing well. However when things got tough for him he complained that George was the luckier brother even when it came to the business of the name change. Traditionally it is the older brother who retains the family name.

Tom the newcomer

Tom, a "newcomer", gave a "performance", said one reviewer after the release of *The Trial of Mary Dugan* (1941) where he plays the part of Edgar Wayne. They went on to write that Tom should not be too concerned about his career because he would be in "demand at every studio" once producers saw the picture. (66) MGM was quoted as saying that Tom was a "find in leading men" and they were going to give him a "romantic build-up." Yet to Tom's surprise there was no 'build-up' instead he found himself playing the villain in his next role and the following eight. (38)

It was because of Tom's "outstanding performance" in *The Bad Man* (1941) that won him the role of defence lawyer, Channing, in *The People and Dr Kildare* (1941) where he played in a cast which included Lionel Barrymore, Laraine Day and Lew Ayres. (67)

At the end of March 1941, Tom made a screen test with Jeanette MacDonald for *Smilin' Thru*. Louella Parsons reported that he was a "dead ringer" for Ronald Coleman. Unfortunately, Tom did not get the part, which was filled by Brian Aherne. (68)

Incidentally, Louella Parsons was the first American movie columnist. She could intuitively sniff out a scandal and her histrionic exposés had the power to make or break an actor's career.

A New York stage producer had wanted Tom to play the lead part in *Peep Show* and had "postponed" production until he was available. Every time a production date was suggested MGM "nixed it" stating that Tom was required for a new film. Eventually there was a lull in work at MGM and discussions began. That was probably after filming of *Lady Be Good* (1941) which completed on 12th April 1941. Nevertheless overnight the studio again "reneged" saying that Tom was required for a "top" role in a very "important picture". The "top" role Tom said was the "half-baked" part of a villainous explorer, Medford, in *Tarzan's Secret Treasure* (1941). (38)

Tom was right about *Tarzan's Secret Treasure*. He turns in a decent performance once more as a scoundrel in this fifth in the Tarzan series starring Johnny Weissmuller. This big budget film was shot at a leisurely pace on location at Iverson Ranch, Los Angeles, Silver Springs and Wakula Springs, Florida between 10th June and 19th August with additional scenes shot in mid-September and another on 8th October 1941. It was released just before Christmas 1941 and would have appealed to a family audience with younger children in mind.

Tom marries

On 10th August 1941, Tom married the lady of his "dreams", former New York model Lillian Eggers, in Las Vegas. Lillian Eggers was about twenty-two and Tom thirty-seven. Tom believed that Eggers was a most "unromantic name" for a "lovely" girl like his wife. (29)

Lillian Eggers was a "statuesque", brown haired, green-eyed model who became *Ideal Television Girl* in America's first televised beauty contest held in a New York hotel in 1939. (69) She was born in Queens, New York in 1917 and met Tom when she was under contract at Twentieth Century Fox. Lillian made three films with Fox, *That Night in Rio* (1941), *The Great American Broadcast* (1941) and *The Cowboy and the Blonde* (1941).

She went on to make two further films, *I Married an Angel* (1942) for MGM and *The Powers Girl* (1943). When being interviewed for *Everyweek Magazine* with other models appearing with her in *The Powers Girl* Miss Eggers believed that a "sense of humour," along with "intelligence, kindness and understanding," were vital for the ideal man. (70)

Tom Conway, the man of her dreams, did have a sense of humour, was intelligent but did he possess the understanding and kindness that she dreamt of? There is no doubt that she loved him very much. She did not appear to have had a problem either with being abandoned by her husband when he rushed to his brother's house at the drop of a hat when the pair would go inventing during the 1940's. Further reference will be made concerning Tom and George's inventing later..

Tom worked for MGM for two years playing bit parts. Fourteen have been listed in his filmography at the end of this biography. Tom himself said he did about ten films but he could not name all of them because sometimes he was not always told the name of the film he was appearing in (36). Therefore it is not clear if there are any other MGM films that Tom appeared in which have not been cited.

During his time at MGM Hollywood did its best to "kill off" Tom in a number of different ways. He was blown up in *Rio Rita*, shot by Wallace Beery in *The Bad Man*, stabbed in the neck in *Sky Murder*, stabbed in the back in *The Trial of Mary Dugan*, and eaten by crocodiles in *Tarzan's Secret Treasure*.

Tom stated that he was at Metro "buried up to his neck," when his brother, George, tired of his role as Gay Lawrence in RKOs 'Falcon' series and refused to go on. George suggested that they allow Tom to carry on with the series. George got out of the series and RKO got Tom out of his MGM contract. (71)

The RKO Years
1942 - 1946

Fig 4: Tom Conway and George Sanders having lunch during filming of *The Falcon's Brother* **(1942)** P.A. Images

There were numerous reports concerning the RKO studio announcement that Tom Conway was to be given an important role in George Sanders' new film, *The Falcon's Brother*. Sanders' character was to be killed off and if Tom came up to expectations then he would be able to continue the series.

When interviewed in 1942 Tom said that he was getting his "best breaks" then and he hoped that the 'Falcon' pictures would be as beneficial to his career as they were for George. Although his career had not been too exciting up to this point Tom was philosophical and put all "detours" down to experience; which was something that one obtained through "disappointments." (29)

Tom's participation in the Falcon series would prove to be a watershed for him. Unbeknown to Sanders RKO had no intention of continuing with the series after his character was killed off. However, to the surprise of the bosses at RKO, Tom's role as Tom Lawrence in *The Falcon's Brother* (1942), proved to be a great success and it was decided to let the series continue. Tom's 'Falcons' were a big hit with the cinema going audience and were to gross more in the coming years at the box office than George's. This was not only due to Tom's popularity but also his acting ability.

Maurice Geraghty, producer of five 'Falcon' films, once described Tom as "one-dimensional" but "full of overtones" and "undertones." Geraghty also stated that Tom believed that he was the reason for the series success and it went to his head. (72)

It is really no surprise that Tom was buoyed by his leap to fame and success with many positive reviews of his films. It proved he was doing a good job. After all, he had only been a Hollywood actor for a little over two years. It had taken George Sanders years of hard graft to get to where he was in 1942. George had smoothed and assisted Tom's path to Hollywood by explaining the potential difficulties before he arrived. George admitted later that he was angry when Tom had more "luck" with the 'Falcon' series than he had had. (73) This shows there was still rivalry on both sides even though Sanders was more successful.

Tom, who was also very competitive, must have felt great to get one over on his brother. At this stage there is no reason for him not to have believed that he would go on to much bigger and better things. His star was on the ascendency.

The Falcon's Brother was filmed in fourteen days from 22nd June to 15th July 1942, which included two idle days with Sundays and one holiday, 4th July, off. George Sanders was paid $14,000 but Tom only received his contract salary. Tom's and the other stock actors' wages totalled a cost of $2,500. Tom was still a relative newcomer whereas George had become a seasoned performer with many films to his credit already.

Jane Randolph, who appeared in the film as journalist, Marcia Brooks, apparently did not like working with George Sanders but enjoyed working with Tom. Jane thought Tom was a "sweet" gentleman who was loved by all. (74)   George was the exact opposite; he spent a lot of time chasing after female members of the company. Tom saved Jane from George's advances by telling him to stop pestering her because she was a "nice girl." (75) Tom once declared that he would never let George embarrass him in front of a girl. (29)

One can argue that Sanders overtly accentuates his character in *The Falcon's Brother* when compared with the Gay Lawrence character he portrayed in his previous 'Falcons'. It is possible but it is not clear if it was done deliberately in order to try to outperform Tom or not. However, the Sanders character in the 'Falcon' films prior to *The Falcon's Brother* was arguably more likeable. Perhaps George was trying to demonstrate that 'B' movies were now beneath him.

If there was a certain amount of rivalry and turbulence on set between the brothers, in sharp contrast, Conway's private life was "calm" and "placid". He and his wife regularly got together with George Sanders and his first wife, Susan, in the early years. They would go swimming, play tennis or play a game of bridge together. Concerning bridge Tom stated he was the worst bridge player in the world. He confirmed he that did not belong to any of the Hollywood sets and had never really liked "nightclubs" and did not have a "social life" preferring the company of a small number of loyal, close friends. He went on to say that he was never bored because he and George always found something to occupy themselves with. At this time they were quite often "immersed" in a new innovation and their wives had "long learned" that they had to amuse themselves when he and George were inventing. In essence he was "perfectly contented" with his life. (29)

Tom and George appeared to have re-kindled the brotherly bond they had forged in their formative years spent in England. At this time they got on very well and were happy in each other's company. However, as Zsa Zsa Gabor would remark, years later, there had always been a definite amount of "rivalry" between the brothers. (76)

Tom moves house

In 1942, Tom and Lillian moved from the apartment they shared with George and his wife to a new house in the Hollywood hills - 1249 Hilldale Avenue. It was about a mile away from the Sanders because George did not allow Tom to live farther away than a mile or two. Conway said that their new house was small but "picturesque." It was a "hideaway" with its main attraction being that it afforded a wonderful view of the Hollywood lights. Tom had come to the decision that since he had signed with RKO it was time to "really live" for a change. (29)

It appears then that in 1942 that Tom Conway was very content with life. He was happily married, enjoyed his brother's company and was happy playing the 'Falcon'. He was earning more money now and life was good. In his mind his career was taking off and hopefully heading for dizzy heights. His parents were now living in Hollywood so he did not have to worry about them being in England facing the threat of a German invasion. He did not go out socialising, preferring the company of family and a few select friends. This joyful contentment showed in his dealings with his contemporaries, in his films and the media.

Tom became very popular with the press and his peers alike. He gave many interviews and enjoyed being interviewed. However, to his irritation, he was continually being compared with his brother. He and George were complete opposites, like chalk and cheese. The Editor of *Screenland Magazine* wrote that Tom was "distinguished", "friendly," "enthusiastic and vital," whereas George by contrast was always "blasé" and "disinterested." In later years, George Sanders fans would go to say that George was the charming and witty one whereas Tom did not possess his any of brother's personality. This has to be contested. (29)

Reporter Irwin Allen described Tom in his column as a "smiling Englishman" because he always had a friendly smile on his face. Allen was not sure if Tom knew that his smile was a "weapon" that was responsible for his popularity with his co-workers. (77) Anyone who has seen *Two O'clock Courage* will understand what Allen meant because Tom does a lot of smiling in that film, albeit a bit goofy; apparently he was like that all the time in real life.

Tom was an ardent sports lover. He was an expert swimmer, played tennis, skied and rode horses to keep fit. He admitted to like watching baseball and football and was "known" as one of the only Englishmen in Hollywood who understood both games. (78) He also liked to get a round of golf in before work. Throughout his career Tom remained extremely slim. Alice Pardoe West reported that Tom said he never had to worry about his figure because his real secret to keeping trim was to eat what he liked but not to eat "too much". (39)

For all his fitness regimes and vitality even in his early films Tom always appears tired, with heavy bags under his eyes. However, in *Appointment in Berlin* (1943), in which Tom's father, H.P. Sanders had a bit part; you can see that he too has heavy bags under his eyes. Tom looked a lot like his father and no doubt inherited this family trait. However, allegedly Tom was an "incurable insomniac" which also could account for those heavy eyes. (79) Another reason could be the fact that he spent many long evenings inventing, designing and building boats with George. A few years later, he would stay up all night star gazing with George using the telescope they built together. When Tom was living with George, after dinner, they regularly spent long hours playing chess together, leaving their wives to their own devices. Is it any wonder he looks so baggy eyed if he was not getting any sleep?

Tom's second film for RKO was *Cat People*, the first of three Val Lewton horror films he would appear in. He was cast as the louche, lecherous psychiatrist Dr Louis Judd. Russian born Lewton always referred to Tom as the "nice" George Sanders. "Horror pays off!" Tom said because occasionally he got a "breather" when he played the 'Falcon' which acted, he claimed, like "a purifying agent." (38)

Arguably, *Cat People* was one of Tom's best films and one of the ones he will always be remembered for. The film is still popular today due to the expert direction of Jacques Tourneur. Tom said himself that *Cat People* was one of the films where he felt he had more of an "opportunity to act" than in any other picture. Originally, Tom explained that the part was "cast as a heavy" but he believed they should let him play Dr Judd in a "lighter vein". His suggestion was accepted and it worked. "The picture is really doing fine business they tell me…in fact it is one of those surprise films," said Tom. (39)

Indeed Tom sank his teeth into the role of Judd and played the part to the best of his ability and he succeeded. He proved he did possess the acting talent that should have propelled him on to much better parts. *Cat People* became RKO's top grossing film for 1942 bringing in $4,000,000. If you compare it with for example, Citizen Kane (1941), which only grossed $500,000, it can be seen how well the former was received by audiences.

I Walked with a Zombie was released in the US on 30th April 1943. It was the second film to be made by Lewton and Tourneur. Tom played broody, sugar plantation owner, Paul Holland, who falls in love with his wife's nurse, Betsy, (Frances Dee). In it, Tom played "Etude in E Op.10 No.3" by Frédéric Chopin on piano. This is arguably one of the only examples which proved Tom's musical ability. Some people argue that his playing is poor but after listening to other pianists, it is believed his rendition is comparable to theirs and after all, he is supposed to be playing it in a sad, depressed way. Incidentally Tom did play the piano briefly in *13 Lead Soldiers*.

Apparently, Tom had never met Frances Dee until he was called to do a love scene with her in *I Walked with a Zombie*. After being introduced, they went into the scene. When they came out a flushed Frances Dee asked Tom what he did when he had been acquainted with a girl for a "few hours". *'He wouldn't tell'* was Hedda Hopper's article headline. Arguably, Tom could have gone on to become one of the best romantic lead males of the 1940's after this performance where he displays great seductive powers and tenderness. (80) "With his good looks and charm Conway ought to be singing to enraptured heroines," wrote Kay Proctor in *Hollywood Magazine*. (38)

A real ship was brought into the RKO studio for filming and it was floated in a tank in six feet of water. A scene, which did not make it to the final cut, had Tom Conway and Frances Dee standing on the bow and a sailor releasing the anchor chain. The anchor fell into the water with a great splash. When director, Jacques Tourneur shouted "cut" the cast and crew started laughing because the plastic anchor that was used was floating on the water. Tourneur quipped: "can I help it if the scrap metal drive took the studio's real anchor!" (81)

It has already been mentioned that Tom enjoyed watching American Football so one can imagine his delight when producer, Val Lewton, called a halt on the day's filming and gave everyone two tickets for the game. Tom tried to contact his wife but was told by the maid that she was at the Hollywood Canteen. Therefore he sent her a telegram telling her that he had "gotten tickets". She was to meet him at "Coliseum Gate Four, two o'clock." Mrs Conway received the wire and arrived at the gate at the aforementioned hour. However, she was not on her own, accompanying her were eight servicemen. The wire she received, read, "Have got ten tickets…!" (82)

The Hollywood Canteen operated from 1451 Cahuenga Boulevard, Hollywood from 3rd October 1942 and 22nd November

1945. It was a club, which offered food, dancing and entertainment free of charge to servicemen and women from all branches of the military. The service personnel's admission ticket was their uniform. Many actors and actresses gave their services voluntarily to the canteen working as waiters, cooks and cleaners. The highlight of the canteen experience was to dance with one of the celebrities.

Tom was ill for several days in early March 1943 with a recurrent bout of malaria. It is not clear how often he suffered from the after effects of malaria. This bout was over thirteen years after the initial case.

In the early hours of 8th April 1943, the premiere of *I Walked With a Zombie* was launched at the Allen Theatre, Cleveland, Ohio. Tom Conway and Christine Gordon attended along with the author, Inez Wallace. Apparently the picture was "launched against a backdrop of eerie exploitation." (204)

The Falcon Strikes Back was released in the US on 7th May 1943. It was Tom's second in the Falcon series and his first in the titular role. Filming ran from 19th January through to early February 1943. One reviewer wrote that this film would "boost" Tom's "popularity considerably" and there was no getting away from the fact that he was the "nicest" thing about the picture. His "suave, likeable, man-of-the-world" personality registered again "effectively" with the audience. (83)

It was around this time we first get a public hint of Tom's irritation when Jimmie Fidler[5] reports that people should stand back from Tom Conway if they intended to introduce him as George Sanders brother. (84) Tom had become very popular all over the world but many reviews and reports always mentioned that he was the brother of George Sanders which rankled him.

With Tom becoming more popular and 'The Falcon' series grossing well at the box office he could no doubt see that he was becoming typed and his acting ability was not being tested. He was becoming frustrated. He may have been warned by his brother not to get type cast. After all, they were still very close. However, George was now forging ahead as a highly regarded character actor who was earning a lot more money than Tom who was still only receiving a stock actor's wage. Tom desperately wanted to play something other than a detective and no doubt wanted to earn the sort of pay packet

---

[5] Jimmie Fidler sometimes went by the name, Jimmy Fidler.

that George was taking home. He was continually being compared to George and wanted better film scripts to deal with so that he could prove that he was as good an actor as his brother.

Nonetheless, 1943 would prove to be a very busy and productive year for Tom. He made a further four films at RKO and gave a number of humorous interviews to the press.

For example, in between filming *The Falcon Strikes Back* and *The Falcon in Danger*, Tom and his wife went on a war camp entertainment tour. It is not clear how long they were away but on their return, their maid had left some messages for them. One asked Tom to contact his producer. Tom half expected that because he was due to start filming *The Falcon in Danger* imminently. The other message told the Conways to look for a new maid because theirs had left to work at Lockheed on the "assembly line." (85)

One day Tom was out shopping in a market near his home. A girl called to him by name and he graciously offered to carry her groceries to her car. Tom went into the store and asked who the pretty girl was. The cashier thought she was Tom's friend because he was so polite and friendly towards her. The girl had told the cashier that Tom would take care of the bill because she had left her purse at home. The cashier handed Tom a bill for $4.65 and 24 ration points! (86)

In his spare time, Tom had been busy designing boats. He had built nine yachts with his brother and had designed a new type of "torpedo" boat and was submitting the plans to the US government. (87) Later that year he told Ernest Foster that he would rather "design boats" than be an actor and the only reason he did not do that for a living was because nobody would buy them. (36) In fact, Tom had been designing and building boats since he arrived in Hollywood. He had plenty of experience, as previously mentioned, because he had been a "yacht builder" in England. (64)

Tom also found time to drop into Chinese lessons, being given by Edward Dymtryk two evenings a week in Hollywood, as a guest instructor. He apparently spoke the language "fluently." (88) Tom never openly bragged that he could speak other languages. He spoke English and Russian as a schoolboy and learned the basics in other languages as well. (89) Apparently, Tom and George shared the nursery as children and learned to speak Russian before they "mastered" English. They were ably "aided and abetted" by a devoted Russian nurse. (15) Tom also tried to get to grips with different local dialects when he lived in South Africa. (29)

The Falcon in Danger was filmed between 13th April and early May 1943. It was Tom's "nonchalance" and "easy going manner" that gave the film a "breezy quality". (90) In the film, Tom, who was a very able skater, was required to do a skating sequence. Unfortunately, he had a fall, sprained his ankle and ended up on crutches hobbling round the set. The scene where 'The Falcon' falls deliberately on the skating rink is filmed using a very unconvincing double. (91) The viewer also gets a chance to see Tom riding a horse for the first time in his very old fashioned jodhpurs. Yet again his 'stand in' is used for part of the horse riding shot which is not very convincing because he is wearing a different riding outfit.

In 1943, Tom was receiving vast amounts of mail from his female fans. Jimmie Fidler was chatting to the cast on the set of *The Falcon in Danger* one day when one of the "studio messengers" delivered a wad of letters and telegrams for Tom. Everyone gathered round and insisted he open them immediately. Tom reluctantly did and they all ended with the same line, "you are wonderful Mr Conway. Can you please get me an autographed photo of my favourite actor – Kent Smith." The rest of the cast had hatched the plan to tease Tom. (92)

A report in the *San Antonio Express* stated that Tom Conway's "portrayal" in 'The Falcon' was "convincing" because he had received a letter from a distressed woman from Mexico City asking if he could track down a man called Pedro who had promised to marry her. She believed that Pedro was living in Los Angeles and it would not be too difficult for Tom to find him! (93)

Tom often received gifts from his adoring fans. One particular Texan fan sent him a real life falcon. Tom trained it as a mascot to sit on a special perch which was placed on the sidelines of the 'Falcon' sets. (94)

Without much of a break, production of *The Seventh Victim* commenced on 5th May 1943 and ended on 29th May 1943. This was Tom's third Lewton horror film. In it, he reprises the role of the enigmatic Dr Louis Judd even though the audience were led to believe that Judd was killed in *The Cat People*.

The Seventh Victim was originally offered to Val Lewton as an 'A' movie. Mark Robson was selected by Lewton to be director. However, RKO would not accept this because Robson had never directed before. They wanted someone with more experience. Lewton would not change his mind so the project was relegated to 'B' status. This was the first and last time that Tom may have been elevated to 'A' star lead status which could have led to the turning point in his career.

Entire scenes were either cut or re-written because the original script was written for an 'A' film which was 30 mins longer than a 'B'. It is not surprising that the critics observed that the film lacked "clarity" and the plot was "confusing". Yet Tom, critics said, played his "usual suave self." (95) *The Motion Picture Herald* commented that his acting was "in keeping with the histrionic standard of the family set by George Sanders." (200)

Tom was interviewed in early July 1943 after he had completed *The Seventh Victim* and gave an insight into his brother's and father's Hollywood careers. Of George Sanders he was at pains to mention that after he made his first film he did not work for "ten months". His father, H.P. Sanders, who had a small role alongside George in *Appointment in Berlin* had been unnerved by the whole experience and told his boys, concerning the acting profession, "you can have it!" (71) Apparently "Papa Sanders" was "upset" when a critic commented that he was not the acting type. (96) Nonetheless, Henry Sanders was said to have had the "charm of his sons." (64)

Tom then took a little time off between filming. On 23rd July 1943, he arrived back at Tia Juana, California which is on the border with Mexico, having spent a short time in Mexico. He was calling himself Thomas Charles Sanders because he was still a British citizen with a British passport. He declared his nationality as "Scottish". According to the border crossing card Tom was travelling alone. (97)

The summer of 1943 was a particularly hot one. In July two weather stations in California registered 124 degrees Fahrenheit. One day, when the temperature was 90 degrees in the Conway household, Tom decided to invent his own form of air conditioning. He stuck a vacuum cleaner in the icebox! (38) (It was one of those cleaners that lie flat on the floor)

Filming began on 17th August 1943 for *The Falcon and the Co-eds*. This particular 'Falcon' is considered today as one of the most atmospheric of the series. The theme tune at the beginning of the film is the same as the one used for *I Walked with a Zombie*. Nevertheless, at the time it was released it was regarded as not up to the standard of previous 'Falcons'. (98) The picture is set in an all-girls school where a teacher has been murdered. Many of the extras were schoolgirls themselves who took great delight in teasing Tom and tried to upstage him and the other actors. On one occasion one of the girls, dressed in a pink negligee, sat on Tom's lap and called him "Daddy"; apparently Tom bolted. (99)

John Todd's headline said, 'Director Has Hands Full with These Forty Beauties.' Tom remarked that he appreciated the girls "fighting spirit" and "determination" to get into the "limelight". He added that the girls were given as many opportunities as possible. (100) There is a scene in the film where the 'Falcon' spanks one of the students, played by Amelita Ward, off camera. In fact, Conway actually smacked Ward on her insistence to make her protestations more believable.

'His Falcon Role Fits Conway – Almost' was the headline in the *Long beach Independent*. It explains how Tom Conway's private life "epitomises" the Falcon role and how he could not find his "treasured" pipe that the girls appearing in the *Co-eds* had hidden to tease him. (101) How odd it was that earlier in the year Tom had told Ernest Foster that he did not smoke a pipe! Perhaps he decided to take it up again! (36)

Maybe it is worth mentioning about Tom and the case of his pipe smoking because it will come up again in this story. Tom, who was believed to have enjoyed smoking a pipe, gave an interview to Ernest Foster who ended his article by stating that Conway had a number of "traits" and nobody would believe that he was an English actor because he understood baseball and did not "smoke a pipe". (36) Perhaps Tom told a white lie here or maybe he did not challenge the interviewer if he assumed he was not a pipe smoker. In fact Tom was always misplacing his pipe and other items at home and relied on his wife to find them for him.

In September 1943, Jimmy Fidler wrote in his column that there were problems in the Tom Conway Lillian Eggers household. Lillian wanted to become an actress but Tom wanted her to be a full time housewife. (102) It would appear, like his brother, Tom expected his wife to stay at home and was affronted when Lillian wanted to go out to work. During the war years many women went out to work by replacing the men who were away fighting. However, the following month it was reported that there was to be no separation between Tom and Lillian because he had agreed to a movie career for her. (103) Nevertheless Miss Eggers did not go on to become a renowned film star. She may have found other work within the movie business.

The Falcon out West or *The Falcon in Texas* (working title) was shot in twenty-two days from 10th October – 8th November 1943. There would have been rest days in between. In this film rancher, Tex Irwin, dies in a New York nightclub from what looks like a snakebite. Tom Lawrence takes a train out west to discover who the murderer was. The Falcon does not look out of place on a horse with Tom Conway doing all the shots himself. Co-star, Barbara Hale, found Tom "charming" like the character he played and noted that he assisted "new actors" when he could and had a great understanding of their difficulties. In the scene where Tom finds Marion Colby (Barbara Hale) snooping on him Barbara gets back on her horse at the end of the scene without taking the reins. The Falcon says, "haven't you forgotten something?" as he picks up the reins and hands them to her. Barbara says that she had indeed "forgotten" to take the reins. Tom had carried on with the scene without stopping and the director decided to leave that bit in the finished movie. (104)

Conway was his "usual confident self as the hero"; in *The Falcon Out West* was the review in *The Film Daily*. It went on to describe it as one of the "best" of the 'Falcons' because of the "added interest and excitement" and made a "strong bid" for the attention of "western fans." (105)

Late in 1943 Tom attended a party hosted by *Photoplay* which was celebrating the renewal of a contract with an artist called Paul Hesse who was responsible for the magazines colourful front covers. "Tom Conway, George Sanders brother", said the magazine had "charm for both."(199)

Three Falcon films were released in 1943 making over a million dollars at the box office for RKO. Is it any wonder then that in early 1944 Tom asked the bosses at RKO if he could be considered to play in 'A' pictures? He was told that his name was not big enough. Tom argued that they starred him with no support in 'B' pictures so why would they not let him "support someone in an 'A' picture." (106)

The Falcon in Mexico was the first in the series where Tom actually progressed and got paid for a film - $3,262. It was still a far cry from the $14,000 that Sanders had secured for *The Falcon's Brother* two years earlier. (104) It was filmed between mid-March and 4th April 1944. The black cat that appears in the opening scenes of the film was called 'Blackie'. 'Blackie' was owned by Helen Holmes who had been a star of silent films. (107) *Film Daily* reported that Tom did his job so well and in such an "ingratiating manner" that the viewer was thoroughly "absorbed" in what transpired on the "screen." (108)

A Night of Adventure "a better than average courtroom drama" was filmed between late January and early February 1944. Conway stars as the brilliant New York criminal lawyer, Mark Latham. It is based on the play, "Hat, Coat and Glove" , by Wilhelm Speyer. "The courtroom sequences in the latter half of the film are rather convincingly handled by Conway". (109) Audrey Long, who played the part of Erica Latham, the lawyers wife, ironically married Leslie Charteris, the author of *The Saint* novels, in 1952. Tom would go on to play Simon Templar, The Saint, on radio in 1951. Sadly Audrey died in London in September 2014, age 92.

There seems to be a shortage of Tom Conway films produced in 1944. The next film he made that year was *The Falcon in Hollywood*. Filming began on 12th July and completed on 29th July. Tom received $5,500 for his work.

The Falcon is on holiday in Hollywood and unsurprisingly becomes involved in a murder on a sound stage at "Sunset Pictures". He is aided by cabbie, Billie Atkins, played by Veda Ann Borg who helps and hinders him in solving the case of a murdered actor. There are a number of suspects including, Peggy Callaghan (Barbara Hale), Lili D'Alio (Rita Corday) and Louis (Sheldon Leonard). However the 'Falcon' eventually works out that the offender is producer, Martin S Dwyer (John Abbot), who was trying to get away with money invested in the movie he is making.

Much of this movie was shot at RKO studios but some scenes were filmed at a private estate in Beverly Hills. Whilst shooting a scene on location Tom told the director to stop filming because he saw a collie dog on the outside of the high fence of the estate trying to get in. He said: "that's my brother's dog. He must be lost or stolen." He asked the film crew to help him get over the fence to get the dog. "Boosted" by the crew Tom scrambled over, picked up the dog and while he was lifting it over the fence a voice behind him said: "stealing my dog, eh"? It was George Sanders. George grabbed the dog back. Ironically the filming was taking place on an estate next to

George's. The funniest thing was that Tom had not recognised it. (110)

Reviewers were not very enamoured with the story line but believed setting the film on a Hollywood film lot was a good idea and added glamour. The film was however "indebted considerably" to the "nonchalance" of Tom Conway. (111) 'Blackie', the aforementioned cat, also appears a number of times in the film.

In August 1944, Tom was on Laguna Beach, California launching a six-foot model aeroplane he had built. He had been testing a "device" to enable land aeroplanes seaworthy in the event they had to make an emergency landing on water. To his surprise he was detained by inshore coastguard officers for suspicious activity. Over an hour later he was released after his identity was confirmed and his "innocent intention" established. (112)

Once again Jimmy Fidler was on Tom Conway's case. He wrote a tongue in cheek fairy tale which told of how there were two brothers in Hollywood. One was a "sour puss" who was rude to everyone and became a "great star" who "insulted" producers who were "eager" to pay him $100,000 a movie. The other, he referred to as "Prince Charming" who had a "pleasant" word for all, was "chivalrous" to ladies, friendly to interviewers and whose fellow workers "worshipped" him. Fidler could not understand why Conway was kept in "B" movies. (113)

Two O'clock Courage (1945) saw Tom starring as (The Man) Ted 'Step' Allison, an amnesiac, who is assisted by cabby, Patty Mitchell, played by Ann Rutherford. Together they endeavour to discover if he was involved in the murder of a producer of a play. Rutherford remarked years later that she remembered that Tom was "a joy" to work with. She added that he "never bumped into the furniture". This was arguably a cryptic comment that implied that Tom was not drinking or was drunk on set when she knew him. (114) Tom was praised by one reviewer who wrote that he acted well even though he was at a disadvantage due to the "poor script". (115)

In 1945, Tom signed a three Falcon film contract with RKO for around $22,000. The first of these was *The Falcon in San Francisco*. In February 1945 Tom was in San Francisco with a camera crew filming a number of scenes for the film. Unfortunately, Tom and the crew went into a military zone to do a scene and were arrested, put in jail, and detained for two hours. (116) The film itself has a lot of action but as the reviewers commented at the time the story is a bit confusing.

Whistle Stop (1946), a film noir, was produced between late June and early July 1945. Tom was loaned out by RKO to producer Seymour Nebenzal. It stars George Raft and Ava Gardner and although it is obviously not a quality 'B' movie it was a box office hit in 1946. In places it is deliberately very pedestrian. Conway, who plays the part of nightclub owner, Lew Lentz, appears very baggy around the eyes. The acting arguably overall is not great. However Tom's "treasured" pipe does make an appearance when he fills it with tobacco and lights it whist talking to Victor McLaglen, his barman, in his office.

The Falcon's Alibi (1946) was probably produced during February 1946. It was later released on 22nd April 1946. This latest outing is very loosely based on *The Gay Falcon* (1941). Rita Corday, who plays Joan, the secretary of wealthy socialite, Gloria Peabody becomes 'The Falcon's' latest love interest. She hires him to help her because someone has been stealing her employer's jewellery and has been replacing them with fakes. Of course there is a murder which the 'Falcon' investigates. In this movie, the ninth in the series, we see Conway bare chested in the shower and then later in his bedroom. No doubt this was done for the benefit of Tom's doting female audience. *The Showman's Trade Review* believed it was a "very satisfactory offering" where Tom continued to be "effective as the suave Falcon." (19?)

Criminal Court (1946), directed by Robert Wise, was filmed from 6th March to early April 1946. Tom plays an excellent young lawyer called Steve Barnes who is running for district attorney. He accidently shoots a nightclub owner (Robert Armstrong) in the club where his girlfriend (Martha O'Driscoll) works as a singer; covers up his involvement but his girlfriend is charged with her boss' murder. Apparently there was a lot of banter between the actors during the making of this film. Tom found himself the victim of numerous pranks and he in turn gave as good as he got. For example he asked Martha O'Driscoll to put his tie straight. He then picked up a soda syphon and squirted it on her bare back. [6]

---

[6] Information taken from photograph author has in private collection of Tom Conway with syphon in his hand and Martha O'Driscoll fixing his tie.

The Falcon's Adventure (1946) was produced from 9th April to late April 1946. Some Conway fans may wonder why Tom's face looks more swollen and puffy than usual in his final 'Falcon' outing. That is because he and Madge Meredith suffered bruising, facial injuries when an inflated life raft exploded in an elevator whilst they were filming a scene. The villain in the film had inflated the raft to "block" the actors exit from the lift. Apparently the "freak explosion" happened when the air compressor inflating the raft failed to shut off. Understandably this scene never made it to the finished picture. (118)

On 28th June 1946, Tom became a naturalised American citizen and swore his allegiance in his former name Thomas Charles Sanders. He was still living at the rented accommodation at 1249 Hilldale Ave, LA. (117)

After appearing in ten Falcon films and seven other films for RKO Tom finally left the studios to try his hand at free lancing in 1946. He had become one of the most typed actors in Hollywood and believed that it was his only course of action to take to try to liberate himself. He was adamant that he would not make any movies with his brother because the "strain", he said, would have been too much for both of them. (119) Was the fact that he did not want to work with his brother because he was concerned about being upstaged by George or perhaps critics would be comparing the two and he might come off badly? On the other hand, Tom, who was always friendly and charming, probably found it tough to work with George who was notoriously difficult to work with.

Tom was very conscious that people did not know who the real Tom Conway was because he had become more readily recognised as 'The Falcon'. Tom elaborates on this by telling a story of the day when he picked up two hitchhikers. He stopped the car, opened the door to let them in and the first thing they said was: "Chee da Falcon man." (120)

In a last ditch attempt to keep Tom, RKO offered him a two year, eight-picture deal at twice his former salary. He thought long and hard but declined telling the head of RKO that he was going to attempt "to break" the Falcon "jinx." For months Tom had been keeping an eye on his bank balance as he waited for the precise moment to make the break. (121)

If he had made a further eight 'Falcons' Tom believed that his screen career would have been over. "Joke all you want" he told the press because he was well aware that he was being type cast and he said that was the most "virulent" kind of "poison." He knew that he was bound to suffer financially to begin with but believed eventually he would be better off.

Here we have an example of a person who was willing to take a risk and lose out financially because he had ambitions to be someone. He believed he had to "prove" to producers that he was as much at home with a "beautiful woman" in his arms as he was with "screen villains". (121)

It remains to be seen if Tom continued to be as optimistic and philosophical about his career over the next few years. Would he break the "curse" of the 'Falcon' and become a famous romantic leading man or would he have to revert to type just to remain working? One can understand why he made the move, however, in two years' time he would be in a similar predicament.

The Falcon flies the coop
1946 - 1949

Eagle Lion, a newly formed film distribution company, traded under the name of Eagle-Lion Distributers Limited in the UK and Eagle Lion Films Inc., in the U.S. It had a relatively small film lot located at 7324 Santa Monica Boulevard. It was a British film Production Company owned by J. Arthur Rank who intended to release British films in the US.

In 1946 Tom signed a "long-term" contract with Eagle-Lion. It was reported that he was going to play a role in *Repeat Performance*. (122) It was also purported that Tom would get a romantic lead build up at the studio.

It is believed that Tom's first film made after leaving RKO was for Andrew L. Stone in *Fun on a Weekend* (1947) aka *Strange Bedfellows* or *Nip and Tuck* (working titles). Production ran from mid June 1946 to August 1946. Tom played playboy, Jefferson Van Orsdale Jr, in this fast paced comedy in support of Eddie Bracken and Priscilla Lane. The film, which was written, produced and directed by Stone, was premiered on 21st May 1947 in Los Angeles.

Tom's first picture for Eagle Lion was *Lost Honeymoon*, directed by Leigh Jason, released 29th March 1947 and starred Franchot Tone and Ann Richards. It is a romantic comedy in which he plays Dr Bob Davis, friend of amnesiac, Johnny Gray (Franchot Tone). An article written later that year in *The Mail*, Adelaide, informed readers that both Franchot Tone and Tom Conway sometimes needed "hangover facials" to "smooth" their "dewlaps, wrinkles and puffy eyes." (123)

Tom was still in receipt of plenty of fan mail but sometimes was not sure if the senders were joking with him or not. He received one particular letter from a lady asking if he would send her a "cardboard" cut out "replica" of his moustache. Apparently she liked it so much she wanted her husband to grow one like it. (124)

Likewise Tom was still very popular with the press. In an interview given by some Hollywood sound engineers who were discussing the problems they had with recording certain actors voices they were asked who they thought was the best male voice in town.

Both men agreed that George Sanders and Tom Conway, who they said sounded "exactly alike", were the "sexiest". (125)

Repeat Performance, a film noir, produced by Aubrey Schenck and directed by Alfred L. Werker was released on 22 May 1947 (US). Tom plays stage producer John Friday. Eagle Lion had initially had problems casting this film. Franchot Tone, who originally signed for the picture, "bowed out" at the last minute. Sylvia Sydney and Constance Dowling were going to lead the cast but disagreements concerning budget and script caused producer Marion Parsonnet and his directors to resign. Eventually Tom Conway was the only actor left of the original cast which eventually featured Louis Hayward and Joan Leslie (126).The problems did not end there for after the filming had been completed and the actors had gone their separate ways some were recalled to do some re-shooting. Tom had to cancel a 10-day holiday that he had planned in the mountains before preparing for his next film. [7](127) Tom may have been going to take the opportunity to take some photographs.

In his spare time Tom loved to dabble in photography. Not only did he take his own photographs, he developed and enlarged them as well. He had his own dark room at his house where he would spend his time developing snapshots, trimming them to size and arranging them into albums.

In 1946, Basil Rathbone gave up his role as Sherlock Holmes fearing he was becoming typecast and left Hollywood for the New York stage. Tom Conway became his replacement in *The New Adventures of Sherlock Holmes* radio series. As previously mentioned Conway had a wonderful speaking voice and was a good radio broadcaster. Some critics argued that Tom did not take the words of the plays off the page. However, he gives one of his finest performances in *The Dying Detective* aired 3rd Feb 1947. Nigel Bruce carried on in the role as Dr John H Watson and the pair performed thirty eight appearances together between October 1946 and July 1947.

Tom Conway, who cleverly imitated Basil Rathbone's voice, was a "very worthy stepper into the boots" of his predecessor. (128) Tom even shaved off his famous pencil-thin moustache for publicity shots (fg 5). Reporter, Virginia Vale, wrote that Tom might be "chosen" to take over from Rathbone on screen, adding that was all without

---

[7] That film was believed to have been *Out of The Blue*.

"trading" on his "relationship" to George Sanders (129). It was ironic though that Tom had to fall back to working on radio and playing a detective to get work. So much for shaking the detective mantel!

Nigel Bruce wrote years later that he liked Tom Conway and he was a "good" Sherlock Holmes. He added that Tom's voice "resembled" Basil Rathbone's so closely that countless people thought that Basil was still playing Holmes. (130)

The premiere of Eagle-Lion films first American made release, *It's a Joke Son,* was held on 25th January 1947 at the Paramount Theatre, Austin, Texas. Among the stars attending the promotion was Tom Conway. On the following Monday and Tuesday receptions and dinners were held and the stars visited local military camps. The group, headed by Bryan Foy, then travelled on later that week to San Antonio, Houston, Dallas and Fort Worth where openings of the film were held on consecutive days. .(202)

Unsurprisingly, Tom also attended the world premiere of *Repeat Performance* held in Zanesville, Ohio, home of Richard Basehart. There was a two day celebration in the town followed by the showing of the film at three local theatres on 22nd May 1947.

At the end of May 1947 Jimmy Fidler wrote in his Idol Gossip column that Tom was "as energetic" as his brother was "sleepy." One morning, just after six, when Tom was driving past his brother's house on the way to the golf course to get a round in before work he noticed there was a large plume of smoke emanating from a chimney. He stopped; luckily he had a key so was able to get in and put out the fire. Tom admitted that if it had been "anyone else's house" he would have driven by without giving it a "second thought." He added that he knew "something was wrong" if there was "any activity around his place (George's) at 6 a.m." (131)

Jimmy Fidler enjoyed interviewing Tom. In July 1947 Tom had been discussing the "habitual sleepiness" of George once more with him. He explained that George went three successive nights without sleep. The first two nights he had been building a boat in his basement. The third night he spent trying to work out how to get it out. (132)

The following year George Sanders reported that he and Tom had sold their $10,000 telescope that they had built together. Apparently "stargazing" had kept the brothers up most nights before they gave astronomy up. George cites this as the reason for his sleepiness especially during the making of *The Fan* when he napped between scenes. (133) Is it any wonder that Conway looks so tired most of the time?

In August 1947 Fidler describes Tom as the "most amusing conversationalist" in Hollywood. He adds in contrast there is no one "less stimulating" than George Sanders. (134) Previously that year Fidler had been on the set of *Out of the Blue* at the Eagle Lion studios where the conversation had turned to "stories that reveal Hollywood". Tom Conway stood up and told a story about a glamorous female star and her boyfriend who, as she was leaving her favourite cocktail club one afternoon, met a nurse pushing a pram. "What a beautiful child exclaimed the boyfriend." "It's mine!" said the girl. "I know because I recognise the nurse." (135)

There is something odd about the above story concerning Tom being on the set of *Out of the Blue*. In *The Showman's Trade Review* dated 11th January 1947 an article states that Tom Conway was "designated for star build-up" at Eagle Lion by Brian Foy the vice-president in charge of production at the studio. Tom had been "cast for one of the leading roles" in *Out of the Blue*. But the lead role was eventually given to George Brent. Tom had been involved as previously mentioned in filming *Repeat Performance*, production of which concluded late February 1947. Filming for *Out of the Blue* began on 27th February 1947 with Leigh Jason directing. (201)

It would appear that Tom was on the set the first week of production of *Out of the Blue* because Jimmie Fidler's article was published on 10th March 1947. What happened to Tom and why did he not star in the film? After considering different scenarios, at first, it was thought that he was taken ill. In coming to this conclusion it was necessary to check Tom's *New Adventures of Sherlock Holmes* schedule because there were not many occasions that he was ill in the early years of his Hollywood career. It can be confirmed that Tom played Holmes on radio on 3rd March 1947 but was unable to perform on 10th March 1947 because he was unwell. This would have been the second week of filming of *'Blue'* at Eagle Lion. Tom did however return to his Holmes role on 17rh March 1947. The nature and duration of his illness is unknown.

Then another article was unearthed in the *Showman's Trade Review* dated 15th February 1947 which reported that Richard Basehart was going to fill the lead role. However Basehart had to be replaced because he was still involved in filming *Repeat Performance*. (203)

After watching *Out of the Blue* one can see that this is film would have suited Tom down to the ground. This is the kind of comedic role that he always wanted to play. There is no reason why he could not have played the lead part as good as George Brent did. The only other explanation why he did not get the part was that he was still involved in the filming of *Repeat Performance* so was replaced.

Unfortunately, even though Tom was such a charming, popular and humorous character his solo career did not take off particularly well. There are big gaps in his work to prove it. In public he claimed the reason his career did not progress was because of the inability to shake his 'Falcon' image. In private he may have started to become very insecure and doubting his ability as an actor.

Bad luck seemed to have dogged him because; in November 1948 he was bitten so badly on the arm by his Siamese cat that he could barely work. (136) It is possible to see the scar left on Tom's right forearm if eagle-eyed fans check out films such as *Bride of the Gorilla* (1951), *Voodoo Woman* (1957) and *Tarzan and the She Devil* (1953) where he is wearing a short sleeved shirt.

In November 1947 Tom signed with Reliance Films. He made two Bulldog Drummond films for them; *The Challenge* (1948) and *13 Lead Soldiers* (1948). *The Challenge* was a "well made" mystery melodrama where Conway made a "convincing and masterful" Bulldog Drummond. His "smooth characterization" was a "refreshing contrast to the rough-hewn interpretation" that had "become customary for private detectives." (137) Tom did make a good Bulldog Drummond and seemed very comfortable playing the detective role once again.

13 Lead Soldiers, a murder mystery, was described by one reviewer as being a "better than average" film which they believed would "satisfy the detective story fans". (138) It was filmed between early to mid December 1947 and released on 2nd April 1948 in the US. Tom Conway "deserves credit" for playing Drummond with his "customary aplomb" wrote another reviewer. (139)

Patricia Clary reported that Tom was to be given the role of the 'Biggest Wolf in Hollywood' when he was to star as Whitfield Savory in *One Touch of Venus* (1948). Tom told the reporter that he may look like a wolf but no way did he resemble one in real life. He stated that he was a "home-loving" and "contented husband". Tom turned in a good performance as the oily, predatory, aristocratic Whitfield Savory who stalks Venus, played by Ava Gardner. (140) The scene where Tom tries to seduce Ava Gardner is hilarious especially when he is speaking on the phone and giggles nervously. The main criticism is that the film would have fared better if it had been filmed in colour.

Early 1948 Tom appears to have signed a contract with Belsam Productions. *The Checkered Coat* (1948) aka *The Fall Guy*, was the first of six films where he worked with director Edward L. Cahn and his first for Belsam. Production began at the Motion Pictures Studio Center in middle of March and ended at the end of March 1948.

The reviews for the murder mystery, *Bungalow 13* (1948), were mixed. "*Bungalow 13* is not a 'B' picture" it was more like 'F", said one critic. It was described as "corny" and degenerated into "pure burlesque". The main criticism being that the cast were looking "square" at the camera and spoke to "the audience". The critic finished his piece by saying that Tom Conway, Margaret Hamilton and Richard Cromwell were "committing histrionic hari-kari." (141) This murder mystery lacked "sustained interest" and suffered from a "poor screenplay" was the review in *The Showmen's Trade Review*. Tom Conway was "satisfactory" but allegedly there was too much "emphasis" on Margaret Hamilton's attempt at "comedy satire." (142)

I Cheated the Law (1949) was an "interestingly conceived melodrama" produced by Belsam Productions. In this film Conway plays the part of an attorney who gets Steve Brodie off a murder charge only to find out later that he has been duped by Brodie who admits he was actually guilty. The film was produced between mid to late October 1948 but not released until March 1949. (143)

Incidentally *The Checkered Coat* along with *Bungalow 13* and *I Cheated the Law* were acquired by WCBS-TV in January 1955 for exclusive, first run, television showing.

George Sanders married his second wife, Zsa Zsa Gabor, on 1st April 1949 in Las Vegas. Naturally, his brother, Tom, was his best man. When the assembled wedding party arrived at the airstrip to board a privately chartered plane that was to fly them there, Tom turned up with a shotgun slung over his shoulder. He jokingly told everyone that he had brought it in the unlikely event that the "old boy" (George) got "cold feet." (144)

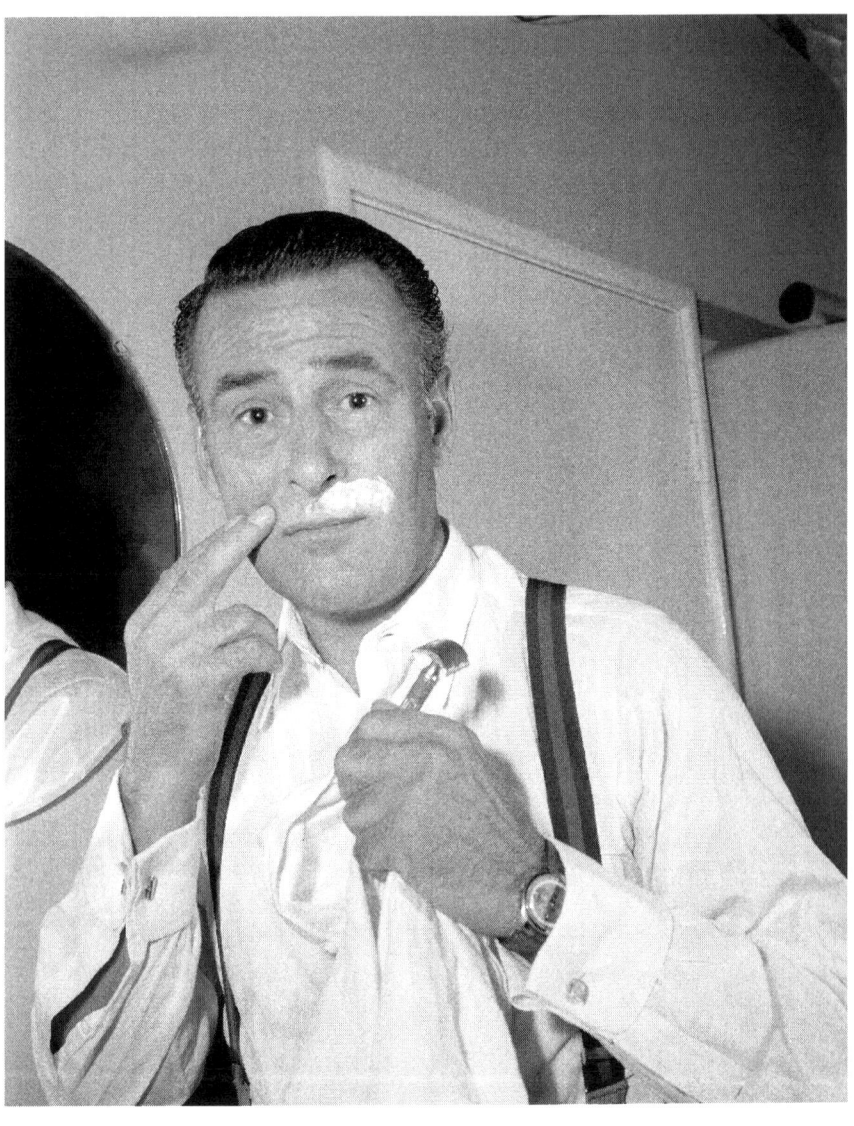

Fig 5: Tom shaves off moustache when he takes on the Sherlock Holmes role in *The New Adventures of Sherlock Holmes.* Circa 1946　　　　P.A.Images

His career was dying a natural death
1950 – 1953

At the beginning of 1950 Tom made the decision to give up acting for a while, in order to shake the typecast image of 'The Falcon' and run his and George's manufacturing business. He was convinced it was the correct thing to do at the time if he intended to resurrect his acting career at a later date. Alice Pardoe West recalled that Conway told her some years previously that his career was "dying a natural death" blaming George Sanders for his inability to progress in Hollywood believing it was his "fate" for having such a "glamorous brother". (145)

He had been disclosing politely to the media that he was frustrated and was finding it hard to come to terms with the fact that he was not getting any work. His brother George was faring much better than him and he was annoyed because the critics were always comparing him with his brother. In private to his friends, he admitted to being envious of and despising George at times. Tom firmly believed that he was a better actor than George and he could have made a better job of the roles that his brother was getting if only he had the chance to prove it.

Tom's last film appearance before his sabbatical was in *I Cheated the Law* released in the US on 4th March 1949. There was now a gap of a year before he was seen again in *The Great Plane Robbery* released 10th March 1950 US even though this film is believed to have been filmed in 1949.

James Mason confirms in his autobiography, *Before I Forget*, that George Sanders wanted to be a "tycoon" more than an actor and he put his "best efforts" into creating a high quality "cabinet making" business mainly for the benefit of Tom. (146)

In the early 1950's Hollywood was going through a difficult time with the advent of television and diminishing cinema audiences. The ease of being able to watch shows from the comfort of your own home meant that television was becoming more popular. Plus, the end of the studio system meant that many actors found it difficult to get work.

As previously mentioned, George Sanders, who was always trying to make money in different ways other than acting, started a high-class furniture business with Tom. Tom, who was a competent carpenter, made more money with this business than he made when acting. The Sanders brothers were making custom built household furnishings of various sorts and television sets. It was ironic that Tom believed he would not have to "worry" about his "acting career again" because their business was doing so well. One wonders if they were making so much money why then did Tom decide to go back to acting. Tom himself cited the adage: 'Once an actor, always an actor.' Unfortunately circumstances must have changed because in the coming years Tom had to work very hard to make ends meet. One can only surmise that like George Sanders' other ventures this one eventually failed. (196)

Billboard, dated 6th May 1950, reported that NBC TV had bid for the rights of the "Boston Blackie" adventure series and were going to audition Tom Conway for the main role (147). It is not clear if Tom did audition or not. However, Kent Taylor went on to star in the role from 1951 – 1953.

When Tom re-launched his acting career at the beginning of 1951 he decided to do something completely different by appearing in *Painting the Clouds with Sunshine*. The film was produced from 26th January to mid April 1951. In the film he plays a Boston banker, Bennington Lansing, who goes to Las Vegas to prevent his cousin, Ted, from marrying a dancer. Tom puts in a great performance showing his range as an actor as he goes from a stuffed-shirt character to a comedic drunk and then a seductive lover. In the final number he even sings along with the rest of the cast and it is possible to hear his fair, singing voice above the others. Tom has a big smile on his face and was no doubt enjoying playing this part. It is a great pity that his talents were not utilised more frequently.

In May 1951, Tom took over the role of The Saint aka Simon Templar, on radio from Vincent Price. The show was aired on Sundays from 4:30 to 5:00 pm. (Ironically Tom had been offered the role of Templar as first choice in 1947 but declined) (148). His first show, *The Children's Crusade*, was aired on 27th May 1951. Conway played Templar every Sunday until 21st October 1951. Arguably Tom's 'Saint' sounds very much like his 'Falcon' character; he does not imitate Vincent Price. He missed one episode on 9th September 1951 when he was replaced by Larry Dobkin, who usually played his sidekick Louis. Tom was allegedly unable to work because he was drunk. He may have had a heavy session after Sunday lunch.

Had Tom begun to drink heavily before he decided to give up acting and now did he find it harder to give it up? Alternatively, had he been a heavy drinker all along? Perhaps there was a specific reason he was drinking heavily on that particular day. Back in 1942 he had admitted that he did not go out socially but perhaps this all changed as he became more popular and successful. Yet in 1948 when interviewed he said he was a "contented husband." Putting it into context Tom was not working very much at this time, this was before he started appearing as Mark Saber and there had been a gap of about three months between making *Painting the Clouds with Sunshine* and *Bride of the Gorilla* with only 'The Saint' episodes every Sunday.

This is the first public evidence we have that his life was beginning to spiral out of control. Tom was unable to hide his frustration and feelings of jealously any longer about his brother's excellent acting career so he decided to undermine him. He admitted that it had been fun making films during the 1940's but the standard of the scripts then were very poor. He had to start all over again and had to fall back on his experience as a radio performer for work. He was in essence confronting his nemesis.

George Sanders had gone to England to film *Ivanhoe* (1952). Production started mid-July and concluded in mid-September 1951. Zsa Zsa Gabor, George's second wife, confirms that Tom was "jealous" of George and took great pleasure in "needling" him. George had refused to take her with him to England telling her she would "spoil" his "fun". This revelation left Zsa Zsa feeling totally dejected. Previously Tom had suggested that Zsa Zsa should become an actress because she was very funny but George told Tom that she was "too stupid." (76)

Tom wasted no time in making his move once George was out of the country. In July 1951 he contacted Zsa Zsa one evening and asked if she would like to appear on a TV show he was appearing on called *Bachelor Haven*. Zsa Zsa accepted Tom's invitation. She was an overnight success and went on to become a star of screen, TV and radio. (76)

George was not pleased when he returned home to discover that his wife was now earning more than him. Tom's provocative plan had worked. Was this a case of high jinks on the part of Conway or was he being vindictive? This is a matter for debate. Nevertheless Tom had plenty of time on his hands with lack of work and the absence of his brother.

During George's absence, Tom was seen escorting Zsa Zsa to various nightclubs, allegedly with George's approval. There are suggestions that he carried on a clandestine affair with his sister-in-law while his brother was away. However, Zsa Zsa does not mention this in her autobiography which is strange because she does mention other men that she has had affairs with.

Tom played Dr Viet in *Bride of the Gorilla a.k.a. The Face in the Water*, which was filmed in one week at The Lot – 1042 North Formosa Avenue, West Hollywood, California. His co-stars were Barbara Payton, Lon Chaney Jnr, Raymond Burr, Paul Cavanagh and Woody Strode. Production commenced on 27th July and finished early August 1951.

Tom, according to Curt Siodmak, showed little interest in the film and was basically walking through his part. Siodmak believed that he was only concerned in going "fishing" and picking up his wages. Siodmak spoke to Tom, and convinced him that the scene he was shooting was an important part of the film. He added that he was depending highly on Tom's acting skills. This "plea" worked said Siodmak. (149)

During the filming Barbara Payton was dating both Franchot Tone and Tom Neal. Barbara had a reputation for being promiscuous and had a string of previous paramours. Tone, who was very much in love with Barbara, did not trust her so he had a private detective spy on her during the filming. Tone's mistrust was founded because the detective did take a picture of Payton and Woody Strode in bed together. There were rumours at the time going round Hollywood that Tom Conway had a sexual encounter with her as well but the allegation cannot be corroborated. Apparently Tone and Payton's other love interest, Tom Neal, both spent time on the lot and in her dressing room. If Tom was having an affair with Zsa Zsa Gabor would he have bothered to get involved in a tryst with Barbara Payton as well?

In October 1951 Tom's television career took off in a big way when he landed the role of Inspector Mark Saber, a well to do detective, who lived in pent house and had a butler. The show ran from 1951 to 1954. His first show was aired on 5th October 1951 and his last outing as Simon Templar, on radio, was 21st October 1951.

Tom had worked steadily throughout 1951 and 1952 on TV starring as Mark Saber, playing 'The Saint' on radio and appearing in films such as *Painting the Clouds with Sunshine* (1951), *Bride of the Gorilla* (1951), *Confidence Girl* (1952) and *Tarzan and the She Devil* (filmed 1952) (1953). He was still working with George Sanders at this time because in 1952 they were marketing a new product in the form of a seat belt for cars. (150)

In December 1952 Tom flew to London to make *Park Plaza 605 aka Norman Conquest* (1953). His parting shot before leaving for England was reported in a number of newspapers at the time. "If you should mention me in your columns I hope you will not refer to my relationship with to my brother, George Sanders." He told them that he did not "like to trade on his name" but "would be happy if you should say that I am related, by marriage, to Zsa Zsa Gabor." (151)

Due to his popular Mark Saber series, Tom no doubt believed he had disentangled himself from 'The Falcon' image. He was now the popular New York homicide detective Mark Saber. Now he wanted to act on his own merits and did not want his only claim to fame to be George Sanders brother. A review posted in *The Sunday Star* stated that Inspector Mark Saber, Homicide Squad was a "Realistic portrayal of modern detective at work." This episode was the case of *The Midnight Murder.* (152)

Tom arrived in England on 31st December 1952. He told reporters on arrival that it was the first time he had been in London for fifteen years.

Fig 6: Tom Conway and Peggy Ann Neilson at Eagle Lion studio circa 1947. Photographer unknown.

A yearning for the bachelor life
1953 - 1957

1953 would turn out to be a very important year for Tom in one way and another. Firstly, he had embarked on what he no doubt believed would be a long and rewarding time, making films in England, now that the Hollywood film industry was slowing down.

By all accounts, Tom stayed in England longer than the six weeks originally reported. He made two films during his stay, *Park Plaza 605* and *Blood Orange* a.k.a. *Three Stops to Murder*. Before he began filming, he did however take time to catch up with his family. He met up with George in London and they both visited their 84 year old father. (153)

In fact, the film *Blood Orange*, where Tom cast as a character called 'Tom Conway', is believed to have been produced before *Park Plaza 605*. Police Constable James Godwin was on traffic duty in London when he believed Tom was filming a scene for Park *Plaza 605* which required him to drive a Sunbeam Alpine Coupe and pull up outside a rundown property. Godwin writes that Conway was dressed in the "obligatory" trench coat and goes on to point out the amount of takes it took to get the scene right because of the mistakes he kept making. It is a very humorous read from Godwin's book, *The Aylesbury Duck*. The only observation to make is that it is thought that the film being shot was actually *Blood Orange* because Tom wears a trench coat throughout that film and is not seen in a trench coat in *Park Plaza 605*. (154)

Blood Orange or *Three Stops to Murder*, directed by Terence Fisher and produced by Michael Carreras was released in the UK on 10th Oct 1953. It was filmed at Bray Studios, Oakley Green, Berkshire and was one of the first films produced by Hammer Film Productions. A worn out looking Tom plays former FBI agent 'Tom Conway' who is now working as a private detective. The confusing plot centres on a London fashion house and two women who wear a 'blood orange' dress get murdered. Tom suspects there is a connection between the deaths and a series of jewel robberies. He subsequently solves the murder but not before somebody else gets murdered. You really need to see the film two or three times to understand what is happening. It is nice to see Tom in his first film made in England but it is not really up to his usual standard.

The other film made by Tom in England in 1953 was *Park Plaza 605* aka *Norman Conquest* which was directed by Bernard Knowles and produced at Nettafold Studios, Walton on Thames. Tom, who is not looking quite so tired, once again plays the part of a private detective. This time he plays Norman Conquest, who you are not quite sure, which side of the law he is on. Conquest is framed for a murder by the head of a jewel smuggling gang, Nadina Rodin, played by Eva Bartok. Nadina, in turn, is set up by the actual killer, diehard Nazi, Baron Von Henschel, played by Robert Adair.

There is a scene in the film where Conquest spanks Nadina. Bartok said that they filmed the scene six or seven times "realistically". Tom put Eva over his knee and smacked her "really hard" and afterwards she was told that it would not be seen in the finished film – the audience would only hear it! One wonders if Tom suggested the spanking scene because after all he had got previous experience in *The Falcon and the Co-eds*! (155)

London in 1953 was preparing for the Coronation of Queen Elizabeth II which was to take place in June. Tom missed the event because he flew back to the USA on 13th May 1953 on board flight BA509 from London to Idlewild Airport, New York. It is conceivable that Tom flew to New York to meet up with Zsa Zsa who often spent time there. (156)

It is worth mentioning that the BOAC Boeing Stratocruiser G-ALSA aeroplane that Tom flew back to New York in crashed on at 0330hrs 25th December 1954 as it was landing at Prestwick airport, Scotland en route to the USA.

On his return to Los Angeles Tom went straight back to work. It is not clear whether there was already tension between him and his wife, Lillian, nor do we know how she felt after Tom's long absence. That answer is probably best answered by Lillian Eggers Conway's actions because she filed for divorce on 15th June 1953, which was granted in July 1953. While waiting for the divorce hearing the Conway's lived under the same roof but occupied different rooms. (157) (158)

Production dates for *Paris Model* (1953) were from 15th – 23rd June. It was released on 10th Nov 1953 (US) by Columbia Pictures Corp. In it, Tom plays the Maharajah of Kim-Kepore alongside Eva Gabor. It is alleged that Tom had a brief fling with Eva during the making of the film. He evidently told her that he preferred her sister Zsa Zsa to her.

Eva apparently complained to a friend that all Tom did was to whinge about his brother's career being better than his. (159)

Tom Divorces

"SAINT NO SAINT" was the headline of an article in the *Sunday Mail*, Brisbane. (160) Lillian Eggers Conway declared that she could not put up with Tom's attitude to marriage any longer. He allegedly asserted that actors were a "class apart" and their careers should come before everything else. Mrs Conway told the court that Tom believed even if an actor was married he should be allowed to live like a bachelor. When Mrs Conway disagreed Tom told her she had "middle class" notions and she was not "sophisticated enough" for Hollywood. On 24th July 1953 the divorce was granted on the grounds of cruelty and Tom was hit with a hefty settlement. He was required to give his wife all of his interest in the family home, 9422 Beverly Crest Drive, Beverly Hills, a car and pay her $5,000. (161)

9422 Beverly Crest Drive, Beverly Hills is a beautiful European style villa built in 1950. The Conways may have been the first owners. It has a wonderful view of the surrounding hills which was probably the reason for Tom buying it. Beverly Crest is a neighbourhood situated on the Westside of Los Angeles.

Up to this point Tom had been living quite comfortably and was beginning to earn good wages; he was doing well. No doubt he believed he was earning enough money to be able to pay off his wife and start afresh on his own. Yes, the films he was appearing in were not that great but he was earning a living. With plenty of work in the offing and the continuation of his Mystery Theatre Tom had decided to move on. With hindsight, this action would later prove to be a costly mistake.

Had Mr Conway always regarded himself as upper class but because of his lack of fortune kept quiet about it? Now that he was earning more was he reverting to type? What is very clear is that Tom's acting career was extremely important to him and it appears that he was not prepared to negotiate.

There are always two sides to any break up. Lillian Conway must have spent many lonely times without her husband who was always working or spending a lot of time with his brother inventing and the like. Tom, who had previously not had a social life had completely changed. Now he wanted to go out and socialise on his own. Could that have been the Zsa Zsa effect on him? Did he perhaps believe that by socialising more it would lead to more work or was he hopelessly in love with his sister in law?

The Conways did not have any children. If there had been children Lillian would have had a purpose to her life and may have been able to put up with Tom's attitude to marriage where he believed it was the husband who should be the one to work and the wife should stay at home. Then to top it all he goes away to work in England for nearly five months. Is there any wonder his wife was upset by his behaviour. Tom was beginning to appear very much like his younger brother.

On the other hand a cynical person would look at this situation, where Tom is acting completely out of character and wonder if this was a put up job. The Conways were drifting apart anyway so why not make Tom appear like a cad and in turn any negative publicity might have been good for his career. The next paragraph shows that that assumption might be correct.

Edith Gwynne comments in her 'Hollywood' column that Tom, who was appearing as Inspector Mark Saber, on the TV was "suddenly quite active – and it's about time!" She added Tom was one of Hollywood's most "attractive bachelors." (162)

Filming commenced for the big budget production, *Prince Valiant* (1954), on 16th July 1953 and ended mid-September 1953. It starred a whole host of stars including James Mason, Robert Wagner, and Brian Aherne. Tom had a relatively small part as the be-wigged, Sir Kay. After watching the film it would appear that Tom is absent in some of the scenes where previously he had been standing next to King Arthur, played by Brian Aherne, when he is addressing the knights of the round table.

Tom is gravely ill

Tom Conway's world was about to come crashing down on him. He discovered in 1953 that he was suffering from advanced, terminal liver disease. His doctor gave him only a few months to live. Arguably he could have been ailing during the making of *Prince Valiant* which could explain the very small part that he plays in it. Similarly he may have been ailing for longer than that if one thinks back to how weary he was looking when he was filming in England. One of the symptoms of liver disease can be fatigue. In December that year, Sheilah Graham picked up on this and reported that Tom was "very ill." (163) Therfore as far as Tom was concerned *Prince Valiant* was his last film and the finale of his acting career.

Tom flies to Italy

There have been a few accounts written concerning when Tom went to Capri, Italy, when he returned and where he went to on his return. It is believed that he only had one payment of $40,000 from his brother George Sanders and that was in either late 1953 or very early 1954. To support this assumption three separate sources have been uncovered.

Zsa Zsa Gabor, who had been having marital problems of her own, says that her estranged husband, George Sanders, contacted her to give her the sad news that Tom was terminally ill. The family met for a get-together and before they parted George gave Tom "$40,000" telling him to go to Capri and "die there happy." (76)

Alan Napier, of *Batman* fame, said in an interview that Tom was terribly unwell and that his good friend George Sanders told him that he was "sending Tom to Italy" because it was cheap to die there. (16)

Tom actually went to the Isle of Capri in February 1954. Harrison Carroll reported that although he was "ailing" with a "liver complaint" Tom flew to Rome because he had some "frozen lira" there. Tom would have probably travelled from Rome to Naples where he could get the ferry to Capri. (164)

Friends became worried about Tom's health later in the year as they had not heard from him for some time, however, Tom's ex-wife, Lillian Eggers, told Harrison Carroll in May 1954 that Tom had corresponded with her "many times" from the Isle of Capri and he appeared to be in "good spirits," and he hoped to appear in a "play in England" in the autumn. (165)

It is not clear how long Tom was in Capri but while there he met a German doctor who was trialling a new drug for cirrhosis of the liver. He told Tom that he just as well try the drug because he was dying anyway. Tom took the drug and it apparently worked. Arguably there would have been certain guidelines Tom would have to have followed whilst taking the drug i.e. special diet and no alcohol.

Tom flew in to Los Angeles on a Scandinavian Airlines System (SAS) flight on 25th January 1955. It was one of the first trans-polar flights from Copenhagen, Denmark to Los Angeles with stopovers for refuelling in Greenland and Winnipeg, Canada. In 1954, SAS had become the first airline to schedule a polar route. It is possible that Tom flew directly from Italy to Denmark or he may have spent some time in England first. It is not clear if he did do a play in England in the autumn of 1954 but arguably highly unlikely.

In any case, passengers on the SAS flights could get a free connecting flight to Copenhagen from any airport. The cost of a return flight at the time would have been in the region of $1,034 and an extra $50 would be payable each way for a berth. The plane could carry 32 passengers, ten crew and had eight berths. A typical flight would have left Copenhagen at 2010hrs arriving in Greenland at 0140hrs; take off would be an hour later and then it would have arrived in Winnipeg at 0805hrs. At 0850hrs it would have taken off again and arrived in Los Angeles around 1335hrs.

Before moving on to Tom's return to Hollywood it is worth mentioning that he was spotted by eagle-eyed, Patrick 'Pat' McDougall, who was working for a Canadian radio station. Pat said: "SAS publicity office made sure Winnipeg's newspapers and radio stations were informed if anyone famous agreed to deplane. Quite a crowd had gathered at what Winnipeggers still called 'Stevenson Field' that day in the mid-1950s when Gregory Peck deplaned and went into the visitors lounge while the refuelling was in progress. Then I spotted Tom Conway" who was "sitting quietly by himself in a far corner of the lounge. I approached him to make sure I'd made the proper identification." (166)

Pat "scurried back to Bill" who had "lost Peck to another interviewer" and told him about Tom. To Bill's "credit" he "knew who Tom Conway was, and agreed he was well worth an interview on the strength of *The Cat People* alone." (166)

"What was Tom Conway like?" was the question the author asked Pat McDougall in an email. *'A very nice fellow if a bit shy,"* was his reply. *"Poor Conway spent most of his career in the shadow of his famous brother, George Sanders,"* he added. (167)

"Every time I think of Tom Conway I get the same mental picture: an elegantly-dressed chap, his face slightly ruddy, sitting rather stiffly in an airport waiting room with those just disgorged from the SAS flight while it was busy refuelling in Winnipeg for the balance of the journey to LA. I saw so little of Tom Conway that long-ago day in Winnipeg: just enough to recognize him as the actor who had made the price of admission to any number of my many visits to my local

move theatre worthwhile when the feature presentation I had spent my allowance to see had let me down." (167)

In February 1955, Harrison Carroll reported that Tom told him that a "new German drug brought about a miraculous recovery," even though he believed he was dying. He was now fit enough to return to work and might go to London to make two films. A further report on 19th February 1955 states that Tom, who had been very ill, "flew in." (168) Strangely, his ex-wife, Lillian, who was to remarry on 6th Feb 1955, met him at the airport.

Never one to let the grass grow under his feet and with an apparent new lease of life Tom flew to London later that month to film *Barbados Quest* (1955) and then *Breakaway* (1955), two Baker and Berman 'B' movies. It is possible that he spent some time in England before flying back to the US to meet up with producers in order to make arrangements for making more films.

It was around this time that Tom spent a lot of time in the UK. He would fly back and forth regularly from England to America to make films. They were not of the standard of some of his earlier work but at least he was earning a living. He had lost a lot of weight and was looking very ill and tired in some of these films. Nevertheless his sheer determination and genial manner no doubt assisted him. There is no way that anyone could knock Conway's grit and fortitude. He was hard working and a true fighter.

In *Barbados Quest* (1955) Tom plays private detective, Tom 'Duke' Martin, who is hired by J.D. Eversleigh, a wealthy American philatelist, who suspects that a rare Barbados overprint stamp that he has purchased from Geoffrey Blake (Brian Worth), in London, is a fake. Blake had told J.D. that he was the manager of stamp dealer, Robert Coburn. There are only four of the rare stamps in existence and J.D. becomes suspicious when he discovers that there is a fifth one in the collection of his friend, Henry Warburg. Tom flies to London to investigate where he is assisted by Barney Wilson (Michael Balfour), a reformed crook. He visits Robert Coburn but he denies any knowledge of the sale of the stamp and states that Geoffrey Blake is not in his employ. Tom discovers that the real stamp is in the hands of Lady Hawksley but she refuses to let him see it. Tom gets friendly with Jean Larson (Daphne Lawrence), Lady Hawksley's secretary. He also finds out that Blake is Lady Hawksley's nephew. He then tracks down an engraver, Gordini, who is implicated in the forgery but he is murdered before he can reveal who he is working for. This is an old fashioned, slow moving, private eye, crime drama which was typical of the films produced in England after the war.

We know that Tom was filming *Barbados Quest* on 28th March 1955 because a Scottish newspaper, *The Bulletin*, reports that he was "badly burned" while filming at the Southall Studios, Middlesex during a scene where he "grabbed a gun" from fellow actor Brian Worth. Apparently the gun went off; a doctor treated his hand on set but Conway, the consummate professional, "insisted" on completing the scene. (169)

On 30th March 1955 Tom had an operation on his hand at the "London Clinic" which would have delayed production for a couple of days. For those who have seen *Barbados Quest* and wondered why Tom keeps his right hand in his pocket a lot of the time all will become clear if you watch the film more closely because he has got a very light covering on his right hand in some of the scenes. It is possible then to discern which scenes were filmed first. (170)

Breakaway (1955) followed *Barbados Quest*. In the film Tom reprises the role of Tom 'Duke' Martin and is once again joined by Michael Balfour as Barney. A very young Honor Blackman also stars in the film along with Brian Worth. The film was shot at Twickenham Film Studios, St Margaret's, Twickenham, Middlesex. Tom looks much better in this film and has put on a little weight.

It is not clear if Tom returned to the US after filming *Breakaway*. He was in England just before Christmas 1955 because he can be seen dancing and socialising with other British television and screen actors at a party at Wanborough, near Swindon, Wiltshire. He is laughing with fellow guests who are playing a game of 'Blind Man's Bluff', popping balloons and generally enjoying himself. At one point he can be seen talking to Yolande Dolan who was married to British director, Val Guest. (171) Guest once said in an interview that producers, Harry Saltzman and Cubby Broccoli, had been considering Tom Conway along with others to be James Bond in *Dr No* (1962). By 1962 Tom would have been about 58 years old so far too old to play Bond. Perhaps if Tom had been a few years younger he may have fulfilled the role. However, Sean Connery was suggested by Guest and he got the part. (172)

George Sanders, who was to star in *Death of a Scoundrel*, was asked if he knew anyone who could play his brother in the picture. He recommended his own brother who was in London at the time. Tom agreed to do the film and said he would fly to Los Angeles after the Christmas and New Year holidays.

Tom flew to the US to make *Death of a Scoundrel* in early 1956. Production took place from early January to February 1956. Tom played a very small part in the film and one wonders if he knew how small the part was to be would he have travelled all the way to America to make it?

Tom played the part of Gerry Monte, brother of Clementi Sabourin (George Sanders), who had been freed from a Nazi prison in Czechoslovakia. Clementi travels to Italy where his brother runs an antique shop which he bought with Clementi's money. Clementi discovers that not only has Gerry spent his money but has also married his girlfriend, Zina. Ultimately, in revenge Clementi turns Gerry into a corrupt police force as an illegal immigrant and he is killed during his detention.

Tom's character appears at the beginning of the film and has very little to say. Gerry looks stunned and wretched as he tells Clementi that he had been told that he was dead. In sharp contrast Sanders is still wearing his hat indoors which serves to accentuate his stature. Even though he was only about two inches taller, he dwarfs Tom, who is wearing a dressing gown and carpet slippers which serve to diminish him.

There was believed to have been a great deal of tension between Tom and George on set concerning Tom's drinking. One wonders why Tom agreed to play the part when he knew there was bound to be a certain amount of stress between them. He may have taken the part because Zsa Zsa Gabor was also appearing in it. However, it appears that Zsa Zsa was not interested in Tom because she got together again with George briefly.

Tom flew back to England in March 1956. He told reporters that he had been making a film with his brother in which he had to say "precisely" fifty one words. He added that "originally" it was fifty three but the film had run "over schedule so they cut out a couple" of words. Here is another good example of Conway's dry wit. On a lighter note, in his luggage that day he was carrying the latest Hollywood brandy flavoured toothpaste. He had vodka, whiskey and gin flavours for his friends. (173)

In 1956, Tom starred in *The Last Man to Hang?* This was filmed at Nettafold Studios, England. Filming began on 15th March and completed on 9th April 1956. He played Sir Roderick Strood, an eminent music critic. Columbia Pictures press office in London advertised the movie under various captions, one headline read: 'HE GAMBLED AWAY HIS FAMILY NAME'. It speaks of his "sophisticated good looks" and "urbane charm" along with the fact that he was selected to star in the film because of his English accent which even though he had spent many years in America had not let his it become Americanized.

A visit, by a young woman to the set of *The Last Man to Hang?* was filmed by British Pathe. In it she meets with the crew and stars of the show, Tom Conway and Eunice Gayson. Tom chats to the woman and gives her a screen kiss. At the end of her visit he pretends to fall over the scenery as he waves goodbye to her. (174)

Director, Michael Carreras, also commissioned Tom to narrate a travelogue film, which featured himself and his son, titled *Copenhagen* (1956). It was a 16-minute colour film. Years later, in an interview, Carreras was reminiscing about the people he had worked with at Hammer Films and among them mentioned "dear Tom Conway" affectionately. (175)

On 3rd May 1956, Tom attended the premiere of *The Swan* (1956) starring Grace Kelly at The Empire, Leicester Square, London. He was captured on film by British Pathe in *Film Fanfare 11* looking tall and elegant in his dinner jacket escorting a young lady. (176)

Tom was once again travelling across the Atlantic to start filming *The She Creature* released August 1956 (US). This was to be the first one of a three-picture deal that he had made with producer, Alex Gordon. Gordon would go on to become a very good friend of Tom's. Tom got a chance to work again in this movie with a former colleague, Frieda Inescort, who he referred to affectionately as Frieda 'tennis court'. Production for *The She Creature* was during May 1956. Paul Blaisdell, who played the part of the monster, doubted that Tom ever smiled but his attitude change when he and Tom worked together. He said that he (Tom) "eventually" gave in and cracked a "smile" which eventually led to "kidding" about and "outright laughs" (177). Shortly after the film had been completed, Tom headed back to England again. He appears to have been enjoying himself in England as he was dating regularly.

It was reported that Tom had been seen in London in July 1956 with Lady Iris Mountbatten, great granddaughter of Queen Victoria, and other socialites. Shortly after this he flew back to America to star in

Runaway Daughters for his producer friend, Alex Gordon. Production started at the end of July, beginning of August. Two days into filming and with one scene already completed, Tom suffered a stroke. He was rushed to the Good Samaritan Hospital where he was given two blood transfusions. Newspaper reports at the time reported he had suffered a "lung haemorrhage" and had been hospitalized on the Thursday night (2nd August). (178) Tom was replaced by John Litel and the scene scrapped that had already been filmed with Marla English. It was at about three in the morning when Alex Gordon received a phone call from Wally Middleton (Tom's agent) telling him that Tom had suffered a "haemorrhage of the brain." (179)

A brain haemorrhage is also known as a subarachnoid haemorrhage, a bleeding in the brain. This is a type of stroke. Apparently, there are several causes including liver disease.

A complication of any type of liver disease is oesophageal varices. Bleeding oesophageal varices are caused by scarring of the liver (cirrhosis). This scarring reduces the flow of blood through the liver. Therefore, more blood flows through the veins in the oesophagus. The extra blood blow causes the veins to balloon outward. Consequently, if the veins break open they can bleed severely. Varices can also occur in the upper part of the stomach. A hospital emergency of this type is one of the most challenging ones to deal with and the survival rate especially in the 1950's was not great. (180)

Wayne Morris was contracted to take over another of Tom's roles in England, as he was due to return there directly after *Runaway Daughters*. That film was *The Crooked Sky* (1956); production of which began at Merton PLC Studios, England on 13th August and was completed by the end of August.

Alex Gordon, when asked by an interviewer years later whether Tom was an alcoholic, said that Tom was ill and had other health problems but did not elaborate. Gordon never actually says that Tom had a stroke no doubt that was something he wanted to keep secret because if the information became common knowledge his career may have been over.

Tom seemed to have recovered sufficiently from this episode in hospital and went on to appear on TV shortly afterward as George Delacroix in Assignment Foreign Legion: *The Baroness* aired 28th September 1956 on ATV London. Produced by Intel Films of London, the episodes were filmed on location in Algeria and Morocco and at the Beaconsfield Studios, Berkshire, England. It is not clear if he made this episode before taking ill in Los Angeles.

Assignment Foreign Legion episodes were filmed in black and white and ran for 30 mins. Merle Oberon played a female correspondent who is finding out about the stories behind the men of the Foreign Legion. She is sometimes part of the story and sometimes narrator.

Later he played Craig Eaton in The 20th Century Fox Hour: *Stranger in the Night* (Series 2 Ep 29) which was aired on 17th October 1956. This series were shortened versions of the original films. The original version of *Stranger in the Night* was *The Ghost and Mrs Muir* (1947). In this episode, Tom plays an amorous author, the same role as played by his brother, George Sanders, in *The Ghost and Mrs Muir*. It is worth noting that Tom's second wife, Queenie Leonard, plays a maid in *Stranger in the Night*. This could have been where their romance started. It is not until 1957 before the press start to mention their relationship.

On 6th October 1956 *The Stars and Stripes* reported that Tom had undergone an operation on 5th October at The UCLA Medical Center Hospital, Los Angeles. They added that he was "resting comfortably" but the hospital refused to disclose his ailment. It is possible doctors were trying to treat his condition. No doubt Tom had completed *Stranger in the Night* prior his operation. (181)

An apparently fully recovered Tom began the filming of *Voodoo Woman* (1957) in mid-November 1956. He meets up with Paul Blaisdell and Marla English again who he had worked with on *The She Creature*. Blaisdell admitted that during the film, directed by Edward Cahn, many of the crew and cast were unwell as they were suffering from influenza.

There was now another gap in Tom's career which suggests he was not too well again. However, he had been dating Queenie Leonard because Louella Parsons reports in her column that the pair looked very happy when they were together. (182)

Tom appeared in Jane Wyman Presents The Fireside Theatre: *Not for Publication*, aired on 16th April 1957, playing Colonel Coldbrace. Similarly he appeared in Matinee Theatre: *Call it a Day* aired on 26th July 1957.

Once again, Tom was rushed to a Los Angeles hospital with another haemorrhage in his oesophagus on Friday 22nd August. George Sanders told the press that his brother's condition was "not good" but it was "improving", according to a report in the *St Petersburg Times* on 24th August 1957. (205)

There is a suggestion, as previously mentioned, that George was not too pleased about Tom's resurrection. At some juncture and it is not clear exactly when either Tom asked George for more money or George asked for his money back. When Tom did not give back George's $40,000, he was very annoyed.

Zsa Zsa Gabor elaborates on this by recalling that when Tom asked George for more money he basically told him he was not getting any more. It is not clear if Zsa Zsa witnessed this falling out or if the story was related to her by George or Tom. However, George told Tom that he was supposed to be dead and he never wanted to see him again. (76) Unfortunately, we do not know what Tom said during this altercation. No doubt he gave George as good as he got. Arguably Tom may have used this opportunity to air his frustrations and jealousies.

It could be that Tom wanted more money to get more treatment from the German doctor that he had met in Capri in order to try to get better. On the other hand George may have believed that Tom would only spend a further advance of money on high living and drinking. There is no doubt that Tom tried his hardest to work and any money he was making was being spent on costly stays in hospital, basic day to day living and taxes.

Nevertheless on 6th October 1957 Tom appeared on TV in the Emmy Award winning episode of *Alfred Hitchcock Presents*: The Glass Eye as ventriloquist Max Collodi. It was filmed at the Republic Studios – 4026 Radford Avenue, North Hollywood. You will have to watch the film a couple of times but if you focus on Tom closely you will see that he sits very still in the ventriloquists chair on the stage. He has one arm on his thigh and the other hidden behind George, the dummy. Tom never moves any part of his body only his lips and occasionally his head. Undoubtedly this episode was one of the best of the *Alfred Hitchcock Presents* series for which Tom received critical acclaim.

Tom refused to give up
1958 – 1964

After his hospital emergency admission in August 1957, Tom's health deteriorated. Determinedly he continued to work because he needed the money and no doubt he wanted to impress his latest squeeze, Queenie Leonard. Arguably, Queenie Leonard was of great support to him at the time. Queenie possessed a strong character with a wicked sense of humour. She was always immaculately dressed, which was probably why Tom was attracted to her. Unlike his first wife, Queenie had a career but he would have still felt obliged to work because he would not want a wife earning more than he.

During 1958, there is no filmography for Tom Conway. The only event recorded is his marriage to Queenie Leonard in August of that year in Las Vegas. He probably recommenced his acting career in late 1958 because he appeared in 'Rawhide' *Incident of the Tumbleweed* which aired on 9th Jan 1959. This was the first of the series and was no doubt filmed in 1958. In the episode he plays English murderer, Sinclair, who is being conveyed to court with other criminals in a tumbleweed wagon. This one was of Tom's best roles. He gives a truly convincing performance of an evil serial killer using his deadpan facial features to great effect.

Louella Parsons commented in her column on the "courageous" health "comeback" of Tom who was now "back on his feet" after several years of ailing from an incurable liver disease. His doctors said that Tom had "conquered his illness by refusing to give up." (183) This leads one to believe that Tom had given up drinking or at least tried to cut back. Arguably, if he had continued drinking heavily he would not have survived this long after having had two life threatening emergencies already.

Parsons was correct. During 1959 Tom found some television and film work. He appeared in *Alfred Hitchcock Presents*: Relative Value which was aired on 1st March 1959. He plays the role of an English police inspector. Shortly after, from 12th April and June 1959 he was filming *12 To The Moon* (1960) in which he plays Dr Feodor Orloff, a Russian geologist. The film is a bit corny and outdated but it was a film of its time. However we do get to hear Tom speak Russian briefly a couple of times. One of these is when he is having an altercation with a member of the crew when he is told by the female doctor that she needs to check him over he says: "Konechno da" (Of course, yes).

Alex Gordon was gathering together a cast of movie veterans for *The Atomic Submarine* (1959) and managed to talk his friend Tom out of "planned retirement" (184). Tom eventually agreed and filming started on 18th June 1959 at Allied Artists Studio at the corner of Sunset and Hollywood Boulevard. There was one sound stage and a series of bungalows. The film was shot in eight days. Some critics have argued that Tom was slurring during the making of this film but after viewing it a number of times the author does not believe that his speech is laboured. The tone of his voice is different from that heard in his earlier work but that could be down to the fact that he has suffered from problems with oesophageal varices or because he is getting older. Alex Gordon recalled that Tom was "with it" and did not "fluff" his lines. (185)

Tom did not retire after making *The Atomic Submarine*. In October 1959, he began appearing in The Betty Hutton Show as Howard Seaton. He featured in nine episodes. The show was aired from October 1959 to May 1960. It was shown on Thursdays and did not fare very well because of opposition on the other TV channels. In one episode, *Goldie Goes Broke*, aired first on 1st October 1959, Tom is using his fishing rod and fishing "flies" as props. This is not the first time he used a fishing rod in a show. For example, in the opening scenes of *The Falcons Adventure*, Tom is sitting on a stool casting his line in the direction of his sidekick 'Goldie' Locke. Similarly, in the *Alfred Hitchcock Presents* episode (Series 5 Ep 35), The Shartz-Metterklume Method, Tom at one point is seated making "flies" for fishing.

It was reported around Christmas 1959 in the *Van Nuys News* that a number of film celebrities had been seen at the Golden Bull steak house, Van Nuys lately which included Tom Conway, Alan Ladd, Ward Bond and Keenan Wynn (186) . So much for the days, seventeen years previously, when he declared that he did not care for the social life.

Too drunk to take the test

"I can't take a drunk test I'm too drunk," Tom Conway allegedly said when booked by police on suspicion of drinking and driving. Surprisingly this humorous line did not come from any of his movie or TV appearances. This real life incident occurred in Los Angeles (187). A week later on 13th May 1960, he pleaded not guilty to the charge of

crashing into the back of a parked car causing injury to its occupant (188). It has not been possible to locate the outcome of this charge.

Tom appears to have been drinking heavily again. He did not have much work and the drink driving incident appeared during lunchtime. He had been drinking during the day as well when he was unfit to play Simon Templar in 1951. However, it is believed it was around this time that Tom's father died in England. It is not known how Tom was affected by this event.

There was one other TV appearance that year for Tom and that is when he played the uncredited, Mr Wellington, in *Alfred Hitchcock Presents*: The Shartz-Metterklume Method aired on 12th June 1960. It is not understood why he was uncredited; whether his name was omitted by the producer or himself it is not clear. Tom gives a good performance as the father who tries to impose his authority on a family run by his wife and governess. He clearly looks very thin and unwell. He had not dyed his hair in this episode which makes him look a lot older.

In July 1960, Tom flew to New York. He had been asked to appear in the stage play, *Sextette,* as Mae West's leading man. He was to replace Alan Marshal who died after the previous Saturday's performance. Apparently, Tom had a falling out with Mae and quit straightaway. In any case, the play was a flop. Perhaps Tom could see this play was not up to the standard of plays he had appeared in previously.

Tom may have decided that now was the time to retire. Nevertheless, he provided the voice over for the collie and Quizmaster in Disney's 101 *Dalmatians* (1961). His wife Queenie Leonard played the part of a cow in the barn. Once again Tom's distinctive voice can be heard clearly with no hint of slurring or hesitation.

Work opportunities for Tom were now very few and far between. He gave his voice for the documentary *The Legend of Mandinga* (1961) released by Columbia. On 24th April 1961 he appears in the TV show *Adventures in Paradise*: Penny a Day (Series 2 Ep. 27). In the latter Tom plays Mr Bartlett, the manager of the Traders and Wool Exchange Bank, Wellington, New Zealand. He looks very distinguished with snow white hair and even his famous moustache is white. He has parted his hair from the left which has believed not been seen since the middle of the 1940's. It is only a small part but he looks very well and much better for not dyeing his hair.

Five months later Tom demonstrates that he still has the gift for acting when he plays the role of Commodore Newcombe in the opening few minutes of the popular TV show, *Have Gun Will Travel*: The Revenger (Series 5 Ep. 3), aired first on 30th September 1961. Commodore Newcombe, an Englishman, is sat in a hotel dining room relating a boring tiger hunt story to Paladin (Richard Boone) who is nearly falling asleep. Tom looks alert, tanned and is sporting a large moustache similar to the one he wore when playing Sir Ian Hunt in *The Atomic Submarine*. Although the story he relates is boring Tom does a great job in making the rendition humorous which was mentioned in the TV listings at the time.

Yet, with increasingly poor health and dwindling funds Conway appears to have withdrawn from public life. In 1962 *The Australian Women's Weekly* reported that Tom was living "in seclusion" and it was rumoured that he was a "very sick man" (189). It would appear that by 1962 he and Queenie Leonard had parted and gone their separate ways.

Tom was adamant he did not want to become a resident at the Motion Picture & Television Country House and Hospital in Woodhills, California. Nevertheless, an observant newspaper reporter discovered that Tom had been a guest at the home in 1962 and 1963. (190) Exact dates and duration is not known. Therefore, he had already had a taste of what it was like to retire but decided that he was not ready for that. It was ironic that a number of actors who Tom had worked with were patients of the home and died there e.g. Frieda Inescort, Bud Abbott, Robert Cummings, Kent Smith, Edgar Kennedy, Cliff Edwards, Virginia Grey and Louella Parsons.

On 11th February 1963 Conway's second wife, Queenie Leonard, divorced him after four and a half years of marriage citing his drinking. Anna Lee, her friend, says that Queenie was very short of money because she had used up the majority of it in caring for Tom over the years (51). Arguably Leonard did not benefit at all by divorcing Conway whose wealth had already dwindled years before.

Perry Mason: The Case of Simple Simon, aired on Thursday 2nd April 1964, was Tom's television swansong. In it he plays an aging, English Shakespearean actor, Sir Guy Penrose. This is a backstage sort of story about a long lost son and a murder of a theatre critic. Tom looks thin and ill with rheumy eyes. In one scene with Perry Mason (Raymond Burr) and Sir Guy they are talking in a bar. Sir Guy tells Mason that he is drunk and Mason tells him that he masked it well. Sir Guy adds that he drunk because he was frustrated. The reason why the Guy Penrose character is so convincing, it could be argued, is because Tom was in fact speaking from experience here. No doubt he had been selected for this role because he fitted it perfectly. By this time it is believed Tom would have had trouble reading his lines because his eyesight was rapidly deteriorating. The only time we see Tom walking any distance in the show is when he escorts the critic, Ogden G. Kramer, by the arm. The reason why he is holding the person's arm is probably because he is using him as a guide because of his failing eyesight.

According to good friend and producer, Alex Gordon, Tom did not have a problem with drink; he never drank on set but sometimes at his home he did drink a little too much. (185)

Tom's last film appearance was in *What a Way to Go!* (1964). He plays the uncredited, Lord Kensington. He stands tall and elegant in a dinner jacket but the viewer only gets a rear and side view of him. Ironically, Lady Kensington is played by his ex-wife, Queenie Leonard. Tom had a brief one liner which was the last words that he ever said as an actor.

Fig 7: Tom Conway aged 61. Venice, California September 1965　PA Images

(Even though he was broke he is still wearing a watch)

Broke and ailing
1965 – 1967

On 14th September 1965 Tom Conway was discovered penniless and unwell in the $2 a day, St. Charles Hotel, Winward Avenue, Venice, California. He was found in a small room lying on his bed, under a bare light with very few belongings. He was dressed in jeans and suffering from a badly swollen left ankle, no doubt a complication of his liver ailment. Two gallons of fluid would subsequently be drained from his ankle by doctors. (191)

A bespectacled Conway told the press that he had found things difficult over the last few months due to nearly going blind after cataract operations on both eyes in January of that year. Mary Robertson, the hotel manager, believed that she had to do something to help him because he could not pay his bill so told a local newspaper about his plight. (190)

Tom said that he found himself in this predicament after making a lot of money. He estimated that he had made in excess of $900,000 gross in his 25-year career and that he made about 283 films. "The roof caved in all of a sudden," he stated. He also claimed that he had been a victim of con artists who had conned him out of $15,000 worth of savings. This admission has to be questioned. If Conway had this amount of savings why was he living in this flophouse? Was this just a story to cover up the fact that he had spent all his money? Unfortunately, we shall never know. (190) One could also question Conway's possible over estimation of earnings.

Up until 1944 Tom had been in receipt of a stock actor's wages. These wages would have just covered his taxes, rent and day to day living expenses which included employing a maid. It was not until his sixth 'Falcon' film that he received payment for a film. Then once he left RKO his income would have fallen. Between 1946 and 1949 the money he made from radio and film appearances again would only cover his basic expenses. He estimated he made around $50,000 in 1952, 1953 and 1954 (191) but after that time the quality of the films he made were not that great and he would have had to pay ten percent of his earnings to his agent. We also know that Tom was short of funds in the late 1950's because he had to continue to work to make ends meet. Therefore his claim that everything fell through all of a sudden could be contested. Also Queenie Leonard had used her own money to care for Tom so when she left him he was already very short of cash.

Still, although Conway had no funds and no prospects as he was not well enough to work; one can see from the photograph in Fig 7 he still has his distinctive moustache. He is smiling and has a neat appearance, even if he has got a little stubble on his face. Apparently he was polite, affable and still possessed his usual charm.

Tom believed it was only a "question of time" before he would be well again. When he felt better he wanted to operate a retreat in Raja, California. "It will be like a sleepy Mexican village," he said. (191) One wonders if he was thinking back to the 1940's when he visited Mexico on a couple of occasions and probably fell in love with the idyllic way of life that he witnessed there.

The only known visitor to St Charles Hotel from the acting fraternity was Lew Ayres whom Tom had not seen for many years. Ayres paid his hotel bill and set about phoning round to see if any of Tom's old friends could put him up. He got a couple of offers but it is not clear if he did go and stay with anyone or not. It was reported at the time that one offer of housing had fallen through. Arguably one of those offers may have been from Zsa Zsa Gabor because she stated that she and her fourth husband, Hubert Hutner, assisted Tom every time he was short of money. Zsa Zsa married Hutner in 1964 and she added that he and Tom became friends. (76)

When reporters asked Tom if his family were aware of his predicament he told them that he did not believe they were as they were either living in England or Switzerland. He confirmed that he and George were not on speaking terms because they had fallen out some years ago and he thought it better that it remained that way.

The scale of Tom's plight was reported in newspapers all over the world. Walter Winchell reported in his column that Conway's current predicament gave "show biz people the shudders." (192)

On 19th July 1966, Tom slipped into a coma which was caused by liver failure. He regained consciousness two days later and his doctor said he was "quite chipper" and was improving. The doctor added that Tom would be remaining in hospital indefinitely. Reading between the lines suggests the doctor was telling the press that Tom's condition was incurable and terminal. Tom had been a patient at the John Wesley County hospital since April 1966. (193)

Around August 1966 Tom went for a three month spell of convalescence in a sanatorium for general debilitation and continuing health problems associated with his liver ailment.

'Future Looks Brighter for Actor found on Skid Row' was the optimistic headline in the *Corpus Christi Times* dated 23rd January 1967. The headline in the *Bridgeport Post* on 24th January 1967 announced that 'Things Are Looking Up For Actor Tom Conway.' (194) These were just two of the headlines that heralded the improvement in Tom's health. Apparently, he had not had a drink for nearly a year. He said he was feeling much better and had a "million" things going round in his head. Tom self-confessed that he "drank too much" however he did not believe it was "a problem". He added, "I just enjoyed it." (198)

Tom was now living in a modern, modest, $135 a month second floor apartment which was situated next to a service station on Wilshire Boulevard, Los Angeles. He was living off his federal pension and a little other income. He refused to say where the other income was coming from. However, the little other income could arguably been from Zsa Zsa Gabor as mentioned previously. Tom confessed that the previous two and a half years had been "pretty rough" but believed his future looked "pretty good." (198)

During his long hospital stay, Tom had to focus on something. He put his mind to inventing once more and came up with a few new ideas; a shaving kit, a secret shaving cream that did not need water and new types of coffee and end tables with tops made out of Mexican pebbles and plastic. He also started making wooden furniture. Ever the optimist, Conway was always trying to find new ways of re-inventing himself.

In April 1967, Queenie Leonard contacted Zsa Zsa Gabor to tell her that Tom was in hospital and was on his deathbed. Zsa Zsa visited him with her daughter Francesca. Distressed by Conway's appearance Zsa Zsa gave him $200 telling him to tip the nurses to make his last days more comfortable. It is not clear what exactly happened next. The following day Zsa Zsa got a phone call from the hospital staff asking her if she knew where Tom was as he had left the hospital. (76)

It was later reported that Tom had gone to a girlfriends house, got drunk and died in her bed. Some reports assume that he spent nearly all the money on drink. That could be contested. Conway would have had to have gotten a taxi or other transport to travel. Realistically it would have been very difficult for someone who was allegedly on their deathbed to get themselves dressed without a member of the nursing staff knowing. Therefore, I believe Tom did tip the nursing staff. He knew that his time was up. He had tried very hard over the years to stop drinking and battle his illness to no avail.

Tom had told reporters that "you just have to hang on and wait for a breakthrough." It is not certain if he knew that if he stayed teetotal his liver may have regenerated itself or if he was waiting for the breakthrough in medical science whereby you could have a successful liver transplant. The first human liver transplant had been carried out in 1962 and the first successful one in 1967. Unfortunately, it was too late for Tom, a very special man, who could light up the conversation.

Thomas Charles Sanders aka Tom Conway died in Culver City, Los Angeles, California on 22nd April 1967 aged 62. His body lay in state overnight 25/26th April 1967 at the Pierce Brothers Hollywood Mortuary. He was cremated on 26th April 1967 and his remains are housed in a vault at The Chapel of the Pines Crematory, Los Angeles. Pierce Brothers stated that Tom's cremated remains would be sent back to England for further arrangement by his family. This did not happen. (194)

Anna Lee says Queenie Leonard could not afford to pay for the funeral so she contacted George Sanders on her behalf. George rudely told Anna that he had no intention of the paying bill and he never liked Tom. Zsa Zsa Gabor remarked that she had contacted George to tell him about Tom and he refused to attend the mortuary to identify his remains. Apparently George was still annoyed about the $40,000 that he had given Tom. [8] Tom's funeral was paid for by the Screen Actors Guild. (51) (76)

---

[8] George Sanders had problems of his own to contend with because his third wife, Benita Hume, was suffering from cancer and she died later that year.

Post Script

A thorough biography can take many years to complete. Just when you think you can do no more, further information comes to light. There have been highs and lows in my endeavour to discover as much as I could about the life of Tom Conway.

Undeniably, as aforementioned, there are some gaps in Tom's life history which only he could have filled. Likewise there are many unanswered questions. He was born into a wealthy, upper class family who had royal connections and boasted nobility in their circle of close friends. He was given as close to an English upbringing as possible even though he was born in Russia and learned to speak that language first.

If his family had not had to escape the Russian Revolution his whole life story and sad ending may have been very different. Tom would still have possessed his adventurous streak and would have spent his spare time designing boats and planes. Perhaps he may even have specialised in engineering in England before returning to Russia. However with a vast fortune he probably would have built his own boats and planes.

Tom Conway was a romantic, handsome, charismatic, charming, funny, well-mannered and some say a typical English gentleman. He was slim, athletic and was always impeccably dressed. Actors wore their own clothes in the days when he was acting; he had great taste in clothing making him arguably one of the best dressed men in Hollywood at that time.

He was a fine actor who had the canny ability to be able to take over a variety of roles left behind by other actors and in turn sometimes making a better job of it. For example, he flourished in 'The Falcon' series, putting in some memorable performances which have stood the test of time and are still being enjoyed in the twenty first century. He gave the 'Falcon' vitality with his own blend of humour, nonchalance, suaveness and charm. He was a good Sherlock Holmes on radio and also had the ability to switch effortlessly between comedic roles like Whitfield Savory and Bennington Lansing to a more enigmatic, sleazy character like Dr Louis Judd to a menacing character like Lew Lentz, Sinclair, or a seductive character like Paul Holland.

There is no doubt that Tom worked very hard during his career. He was working steadily throughout the 1940's until he decided to part with RKO. He hoped that he would be able to forge ahead as a freelancer, land better roles and not have to play the part of a detective anymore. Nevertheless, he was a realist and did not have any illusions about the acting business. He knew his career could fizzle out at any time.

By the end of the 1940's his film appearances were few and far between. Why? This was the end of the golden era of Hollywood. The studio system came to an end at the end of the 1940's and there were lots of out of work actors trying to find work, plus TV was now becoming the popular new medium.

After his career break Tom made himself available for all types of work and expanded his CV by turning to television for work. He became famous in the 1950's for his portrayal of Mark Saber and put in excellent performances as Max Collodi and Sinclair. He received a Hollywood Walk of Fame Star for his contribution to television in 1960; it is located at 1617 Vine Street.

Tom may have gone on to be a renowned actor but he was unlucky; he did not get the breaks. He could have gone to New York and been a success on stage in *Peep Show* but that did not happen, MGM nixed that. MGM were going to build him up for a leading male role but did not. RKO refused to put him in 'A' pictures because his name was not big enough! *Seventh Victim* had originally been slated as an 'A' movie but was demoted to a 'B' film when Val Lewton refused to offer the job of producer to an 'A' director. It was also suggested that Eagle Lion were going to give Tom a romantic lead build up but did not.

During the 1940's Tom was very active. Not only was he making a lot of pictures he also had time to undertake many activities such as boat and aeroplane design and building. His other interests included sailing, swimming, riding, golf, photography, fishing, tennis, skiing and inventing. He was very close to his brother, George Sanders, who he spent a lot of time with in the early days.

Something happened to change all this. Movie work dried up for Tom but George continued to forge ahead with his career. George helped Tom by suggesting they start a high class furniture business together. Tom gave up being an actor and ran the business because of his knowledge of carpentry. During this time George had starred in *All about Eve* and subsequently won an Oscar. It was not long after this that Tom returned to being an actor. It is not clear if the furniture business folded or if Tom was just jealous because George had won an award.

It is not inconceivable that the more envious and exasperated that Tom got the more he drank. Nevertheless Tom re-invented himself and worked very hard during the 1950's even though he was suffering from cirrhosis of the liver. He had many setbacks and hospital visits over the last fourteen years of his life. Towards the end of his life he began inventing again, he was completely off the wagon and was looking forward to starting again even if it would be a cold start. He never moaned about his situation and did not publicly bear any kind of grudge against his brother.

In conclusion when Tom was ill or short of money he hid himself away. For example on his return to England in 1929 he secreted himself in a hotel in 'Liverpool' instead of going home. When he was initially diagnosed with terminal liver disease he went to Capri to die alone. Then when he was ill and broke in 1962 he lived "in seclusion" and finally he hid away a in a cheap hotel in Venice, California waiting to die.

In the end he opted to die in the arms of a loved one rather than in the clinical surroundings of a hospital and alone. He had possibly got to the stage where he did not want to suffer any longer. Knowing the state of his liver he would have been well aware that a large amount of alcohol imbibed at one session would have had a detrimental effect on it.

Tom Conway's Filmography

Tom Conway's film career spanned from 1940 to 1964. He featured in around 63 films, taking the leading role in around twenty-seven. He acted for the likes Fred Zinnemann, William Wyler, Jacques Tourneur, Anthony Mann, Terence Fisher and Michael Carreras. His male co-stars ranged from Lionel Barrymore, Robert Young, Robert Cummings, Louis Hayward, Lew Ayres, Wallace Beery, George Raft, James Mason, George Sanders, Walter Pidgeon, Johnny Weissmuller, Brian Aherne, Raymond Burr, Van Heflin and Ronald Reagan. His leading ladies ranged from Ava Gardner, Greer Garson, Laraine Day, Ann Rutherford, Frances Dee, Kathryn Grayson, Barbara Payton, Eva Gabor, Eva Bartok, Virginia Mayo, Eunice Gayson, Zsa Zsa Gabor, Maureen O'Sullivan and Eleanor Powell.

1940

Waterloo Bridge
108 mins
MGM
Producer: Sidney Franklin
Director: Mervyn LeRoy
Screenplay: S.N. Behman, Hans Rameau, George Froeschel
Narrator: Tom Conway (uncredited)
Cast: Vivien Leigh, Robert Taylor, Lucile Watson, Virginia Field.

The Great Meddler
Short
MGM
Director: Fred Zinnemann
Original story: Joseph Ansen
Screenplay: Barney Gerard
Screenplay: Julian Hochfelder
Cast: Tom Conway

1941

Sky Murder
72 Mins
MGM
Producer: Frederick Stephani
Director: George B. Seitz
Screenplay: William R. Lipman
Cast: Walter Pidgeon, Donald Meek, Karen Verne, Edward Ashley, Joyce Compton, Tom Conway.

The Wild Man of Borneo
78 Mins
MGM
Producer: Joseph L. Mankiewicz
Director: Robert B. Sinclair
Screenplay: Waldo Salt, John McClain
Cast: Frank Morgan, Mary Howard, Billie Burke, Donald Meek, Bonita Granville, Dan Dailey. Phil Silvers. Tom Conway (uncredited actor in film scene)

The Trial of Mary Dugan
87 Mins
MGM
Producer: Edwin H. Knopf
Director: Norman Z. Mcleod.
Writer: Bayard Veiller
Cast: Laraine Day, Robert Young, Tom Conway, Frieda Inescourt, Henry O'Neill, John Litel, Marsha Hunt.

Free and Easy
56 Mins
MGM
Producer: Milton H. Bren
Director: George Sidney, Edward Buzzell (uncredited)
Writer: Ivor Novello
Screenplay: Marvin Borowosky
Cast: Robert Cummings, Ruth Hussey, Judith Anderson, C. Aubrey Smith, Nigel Bruce, Reginald Owen, Tom Conway, Forrester Harvey.

The Bad Man
70 Mins
MGM
Producer: J. Walter Ruben
Director: Richard Thorpe
Screenplay: Wells Root
Cast: Wallace Beery, Lionel Barrymore, Laraine Day, Ronald Reagan, Henry Travers, Chris-Pin Martin, Tom Conway, Chill Wills, Nydia Westman

The People vs. Dr. Kildare
78 mins
MGM
Director: Harold S. Bucquet
Screenplay: William Goldbeck, Harry Ruskin.
Cast: Lew Ayres, Lionel Barrymore, Laraine Day, Bonita Granville, Alma Kruger, Red Skelton, Paul Stanton, Diana Lewis, Walter Kingsford, Neil Craig, Tom Conway, Marie Blake, Eddie Acuff, George Reed.

Lady Be Good
112 Mins
MGM
Producer: Arthur Freed
Director: Norman Z. McLeod, Busby Berkeley (uncredited)
Screenplay: Jack McGowan, Kay Van Riper, John McClain
Cast: Eleanor Powell, Ann Sothern, Robert Young, Lionel Barrymore, John Carroll, Red Skelton, Virginia O'Brien, Tom Conway, Dan Dailey.

Tarzan's Secret Treasure
81 mins
MGM
Producer: B. P. Fineman
Director: Richard Thorpe
Screenplay: Myles Connolly, Paul Gangelin.
Cast: Johnny Weissmuller, Maureen O'Sullivan, Johnny Sheffield, Reginald Owen, Barry Fitzgerald, Tom Conway, Philip Dorn, Cordell Hickman.

1942

Mr and Mrs North
67 mins
MGM
Producer: Irving Asher
Director: Robert S. Sinclair
Screenplay: S.K. Lauren
Cast: Gracie Allen, William Post Jr, Paul Kelly, Rose Hobart, Virginia Grey, Tom Conway, Felix Bressart, Stuart Crawford, Porter Hall, Millard Mitchell, Lucien Littlefield, Inez Cooper, Keye Luke.

Rio Rita
91 mins
MGM
Producer: Pandro S. Berman
Director: S. Sylvan Simon
Screenplay: Richard Connell, Gladys Lehman.
Cast: Bud Abbott, Lou Costello, Kathryn Grayson, John Carroll, Patricia Dane, Tom Conway, Peter Whitney, Barry Nelson, Arthur Space, Dick Rich.

Grand Central Murder
73 mins
MGM
Producer: B. P. Zeidman
Director: S. Sylvan Simon
Screenplay: Peter Ruric
Cast: Van Heflin, Patricia Dane, Virginia Grey, Samuel S. Hinds, Sam Levene, Connie Gilchrist, Mark Daniels, Stephen McNally, Tom Conway, Betty Wells, George Lynn, Roman Bohnen, Millard Mitchell.

Mrs Miniver
134 mins
MGM
Producer: Sidney Franklin, William Wyler (as a William Wyler Production)
Director: William Wyler
Screenplay: Arthur Wimperis, George Froeschel, James Hilton, Claudine West.
Cast: Greer Garson, Walter Pidgeon, Teresa Wright, Dame May Whitty, Reginald Owen, Henry Travers, Richard Ney, Henry Wilcoxon, Christopher Severn, Brenda Forbes, Chris Sanders, Maria De Becker, Helmut Dantine, John Abbott, Connie Leon, Rhys Willis, Tom Conway.

The Falcon's Brother
63 mins
RKO
Producer: Maurice Geraghty
Director: Stanley Logan
Screenplay: Stuart Palmer, Craig Rice.
Cast: George Sanders, Tom Conway, Jane Randolph, Don Barclay, Cliff Clark, Edward Gargan, Eddie Dunn, Charlotte Wynters, James Newill, Keye Luke, Amanda Varela, George J. Lewis, Gwili Andre.

Cat People
73 mins
RKO
Producer: Val Lewton
Director: Jacques Tourneur
Writer: Dewitt Bodeen
Cast: Simone Simon, Kent Smith, Tom Conway, Jane Randolph, Jack Holt.

1943

The Falcon Strikes Back
66 mins
RKO
Producer: Maurice Geraghty
Director: Edward Dmytryk
Screenplay: Edward Dein, Gerald Geraghty.
Cast: Tom Conway, Harriet Hillard, Jane Randolph, Edgar Kennedy, Cliff Edwards, Rita Corday, Erford Gage, Wynne Gibson, Andre Charlot, Richard Loo, Cliff Clark, Edward Gargan.

I Walked with a Zombie
69 mins
RKO
Producer: Val Lewton
Director: Jacques Tourneur
Screenplay: Curt Siodmak, Ardel Wray.
Cast: James Ellison, Frances Dee, Tom Conway, Edith Barrett, James Bell, Christine Gordon, Theresa Harris, Sir Lancelot, Darby Jones, Jeni Le Gon.

The Falcon in Danger
69 mins
RKO
Producer: Maurice Geraghty
Director: William Clemens
Screenplay: Fred Niblo Jr, Craig Rice.
Cast: Tom Conway, Jean Brooks, Elaine Shepard, Amelita Ward, Cliff Clark, Edward Gargan, Clarence Kolb, Felix Basch, Richard Davies, Richard Martin, Erford Gage, Eddie Dunn.

The Seventh Victim
71 mins
RKO
Producer: Val Lewton
Director: Mark Robson
Screenplay: Charles O'Neal, DeWitt Bodeen.
Cast: Tom Conway, Jean Brooks, Isabel Jewell, Kim Hunter, Evelyn Brent, Erford Gage, Ben Bard, Hugh Beaumont, Chef Milani, Marguerita Sylva.

The Falcon and the Co-eds
67 mins
RKO
Producer: Maurice Geraghty
Director: William Clemens
Screenplay: Ardel Wray, Gerald Geraghty.
Cast: Tom Conway, Jean Brooks, Rita Corday, Amelita Ward, Isabel Jewell, George Givot, Cliff Clark, Edward Gargan, Barbara Brown, Nita Hunter, Ruth Alverez, Nancy, McCollum, Patti Brill, Olin Howland.

1944

The Falcon out West
64 mins
RKO
Producer: Maurice Geraghty
Director: William Clemens
Screenplay: Billy Jones, Morton Grant.
Cast: Tom Conway, Carole Gallagher, Barbara Hale, Joan Barclay, Minor Watson, Donald Douglas, Lyle Talbot, Lee Trent, Perc Launders.

A Night of Adventure
65 mins
RKO
Producer: Herman Schlom
Director: Gordon Douglas
Screenplay: Crane Wilbur, Wilhelm Speyer.
Cast: Tom Conway, Audrey Long, Edward Brophy, Louis Borel, Addison Richards, Jean Brooks, Nancy Gates, Russell Hopton, Claire Carleton, Emory Parnell, Edmund Glover.

The Falcon in Mexico
70 mins
RKO
Producer: Maurice Geraghty
Director: William Berke.
Screenplay: George Worthing Yates, Gerald Geraghty.
Cast: Tom Conway, Mona Maris, Martha Vickers, Nestor Paiva, Mary Currier, Cecilia Callejo, Emory Parnell, Joseph Vitale, Pedro de Cordoba, Fernando Alverado, Bryant Washburn.

The Falcon in Hollywood
67 mins
RKO
Producer: Maurice Geraghty
Director: Gordon Douglas
Screenplay: Gerald Geraghty
Cast: Tom Conway, Barbara Hale, Veda Ann Borg, John Abbott, Sheldon Leonard, Konstantin Sheyne, Emory Parnell, Frank Jenks, Jean Brooks, Rita Corday, Walter Soderling, Useff Ali, Robert Clark.

1945

Two O'clock Courage
68 mins
RKO
Producer: Benjamin Stoloff
Director: Anthony Mann
Screenplay: Robert E. Kent
Cast: Tom Conway, Ann Rutherford, Richard Lane, Lester Matthews, Roland Drew, Emory Parnell, Jean Brooks.

The Falcon in San Francisco
66 mins
RKO
Producer: Maurice Geraghty
Director: Joseph H. Lewis
Screenplay: Robert E. Kent, Ben Markson
Cast: Tom Conway, Rita Corday, Edward Brophy, Sharyn Moffett, Fay Helm, Robert Armstrong, Carl Kent, George Holmes, John Mylong.

1946

Whistle Stop
85 mins
Nero Films released through United Artists
Producer: Seymour Nebenzal
Director: Leonide Moguy
Screenplay: Philip Yordan
Cast: George Raft, Ava Gardner, Victor McLaglen, Tom Conway, Jorja Curthright, Jane Nigh, Florence Bates, Charles Drake, Carmel Myers, Jimmy Ames, Mack Gray.

The Falcon's Alibi
61 mins
RKO
Producer: William Berke
Director: Ray McCarey
Screenplay: Paul Yawitz
Cast: Tom Conway, Rita Corday, Vince Barnett, Jane Greer, Elisha Cook Jr., Emory Parnell, Al Bridge, Esther Howard, Jean Brooks, Paul Brooks, Jason Robards Sr., Morgan Wallace, Lucien Prival.

Criminal Court
60 mins
RKO
Producer: Martin Mooney
Director: Robert Wise
Screenplay: Lawrence Kimble
Cast: Tom Conway, Martha O'Driscoll, June Clayworth, Robert Armstrong, Addison Richards, Pat Gleason, Steve Brodie, Robert Warwick, Phil Warren, Joe Devlin, Lee Bonnell, Robert Clarke.

The Falcon's Adventure
61 mins
RKO
Producer: Herman Schlom
Director: William Berke
Screenplay: Aubrey Wisberg, Robert E. Kent (additional dialogue)
Cast: Tom Conway, Madge Meredith, Edward Brophy, Robert Warwick, Myrna Dell, Steve Brodie, Ian Wolfe, Carol Forman, Joseph Crehan, Phil Warren, Tony Barrett, Harry Harvey, Jason Robards Sr.

1947

Lost Honeymoon
71 mins
Eagle-Lion (USA)
Eagle-Lion Distributors Limited (UK)
Producer: Lee S. Marcus
Director: Leigh Jason
Screenplay: Joseph Fields
Cast: Franchot Tone, Ann Richards, Tom Conway, Frances Rafferty, Clarence Kolbe, Una O'Connor, Winston Severn.

Fun on a Weekend
93 mins
Andrew L. Stone Productions.
Distributors: United Artists
Producer: Andrew L. Stone
Director: Andrew L. Stone
Screenplay: Andrew L. Stone
Cast: Eddie Bracken, Pricilla Lane, Tom Conway, Allen Jenkins, Arthur Treacher, Clarence Kolb, Alma Kruger, Russell Hicks, Fritz Feld.

Repeat Performance
91 mins
Aubrey Schenk Productions
Distributors: Eagle-Lion (USA)
Eagle-Lion Distributors Limited (UK)
Producer: Aubrey Schenck
Director: Alfred L. Werker
Screenplay: Walter Bullock
Cast: Louis Hayward, Joan Leslie, Virginia Field, Tom Conway, Richard Basehart, Natalie Schafer, Benay Venuta, Ilka Gruning.

1948

13 Lead Soldiers
64 mins
Bernard Small Productions
Distributors: Twentieth Century Fox Film Corporation
Producer: Bernard Small
Director: Frank McDonald
Screenplay: Irving Elman
Cast: Tom Conway, John Newland, Maria Palmer, Helen Westcott, William Sterling, Terry Kilburn, Gordon Richards, John Goldsworthy.

The Challenge
68 mins
Bernard Small Productions
Distributors: Twentieth Century Fox Film Corporation
Producer: Bernard Small
Director: Jean Yarbrough
Screenplay: Irving Elman, Frank Gruber
Cast: Tom Conway, June Vincent, Richard Wyler, John Newland, Elly Mlyon, Houseley Stevenson, Terry Kilburn, Stanley Logan, Leyland Hodgson, James Fairfax, Patrick Aherne, Oliver Blake.

The Checkered Coat
66 mins
Belsam Productions Inc.
Distributor: Twentieth Century Fox Corporation
Producer: Sam Baerwitz
Director: Edward L. Cahn
Screenplay: Merwin Gerard, John C. Higgins, Seeleg Lester.
Cast: Tom Conway, Noreen Nash, Hurd Hatfield, James Seay, Garry Owen, Marten Lamont, Frank Cady, Leonard Mudie, Russell Arms, Lee Bonnell.

One Touch of Venus
82 mins
Artists Alliance
Universal International Pictures
Distributor: Universal Pictures
Producer: Lester Cowan, William A. Seiter
Director: William A. Seiter

Screenplay: Harry Kurnitz, Frank Tashlin
Cast: Robert Walker, Ava Gardner, Dick Haymes, Eve Arden, Olga San Juan, Tom Conway, James Flavin, Sara Allgood.

Bungalow 13
70 mins
Belsam Productions Inc.
Distributor: Twentieth Century Fox Corporation
Producer: Sam Baerwitz
Director: Edward L. Cahn
Screenplay: Sam Baerwitz, Richard G. Hubler
Cast: Tom Conway, Margaret Hamilton, Richard Cromwell, James Flavin, Marjorie Hoshelle, Frank Cady, Eddie Acuff, Jody Gilbert, Juan Varro.

1949

I Cheated the Law
69 mins
Belsam Productions Inc.
Distributor: Twentieth Century Fox Corporation
Producer: Sam Baerwitz
Director: Edward L. Cahn
Screenplay: Sam Baerwitz, Richard G. Huber
Cast: Tom Conway, Steve Brodie, Robert Osterloh, Barbara Billingsley, Russell Hicks, James Seay, Chet Huntley, Tommy Noonan, William Gould.

1950

The Great Plane Robbery
61 mins
Belsam Productions Inc.
Distributor: Twentieth Century Fox Corporation
Producer: Sam Baerwitz
Director: Edward L. Cahn
Screenplay: Sam Baerwitz, Clarence Green, Richard G. Hubler, Russell Rouse.
Cast: Tom Conway, Margaret Hamilton, Steve Brodie, Lynne Roberts, David Bruce, Marcel Journet, Gil Frye, Ralph Dunn, Lucille Barkley

1951

Painting the Clouds with Sunshine
87 mins

Warner Brothers
Producer: William Jacobs
Director: David Butler
Screenplay: Harry Clork, Roland Kibbee, Peter Milne
Cast: Dennis Morgan, Gene Nelson, Lucille Norman, S.Z. Sakall, Virginia Mayo, Tom Conway, Wallace Ford.

Bride of the Gorilla
70 mins
Jack Broder Productions Inc.
Producer: Edward Leven, Jack Broder
Director: Curt Siodmak
Screenplay: Curt Siodmak
Cast: Barbara Payton, Lon Chaney Jr., Raymond Burr, Tom Conway, Paul Cavanagh, Gisela Werbisek, Carol Varga, Paul Maxey, Woody Strode.

1952

Confidence Girl
81 mins
Andrew L. Stone Productions
Producer: Andrew L. Stone
Director: Andrew L. Stone
Screenplay: Andrew L. Stone
Cast: Tom Conway, Hilary Brooke, Eddie Marr, John Gallaudet, Jack Kruschen, Dan Riss, Walter Kingsford, Paul Livermore, Aline Towne, Helen Van Tuyl, Edmund Cobb, Truman Bradley, Leo Cleary, Roy Engel.

1953

Peter Pan
77 mins
Walt Disney Productions
Producer: Walt Disney
Directors: Clyde Geronimi, Wilfred Jackson, Hamilton Luske, Jack Kinney
Writer: J. M. Barrie
Narrator: Tom Conway
Cast: Bobby Driscoll, Kathryn Beaumont, Hans Conried, Bill Thompson, Heather Angel, Paul Collins, Tommy Luske, Candhy Candido.

Tarzan and the She Devil
75 mins
Sol Lesser Production
Distributor: RKO
Producer: Sol Lessur
Director: Kurt Neumann
Screenplay: Karl Kamb, Carroll Young
Cast: Lex Barker, Joyce Mackenzie, Raymond Burr, Tom Conway, Michael Granger, Henry Brandon.

Park Plaza 605
Norman Conquest (US)
75 Mins
B & A Productions
Producer: Albert Fennell, Bertram Ostrer
Director: Bernard Knowles
Screenplay: Bertram Ostrer, Albert Fennell, Bernard Knowles
Cast: Tom Conway, Eva Bartok, Joy Shelton, Sidney James, Richard Wattis, Carl Jaffe, Frederick Schiller, Robert Adair, Anton Diffring, Ian Fleming.

Blood Orange
Three Stops to Murder (US)
76 minas
Hammer Film Productions
Producer: Michael Carreras
Director: Terence Fisher
Writer: Jan Read
Cast: Tom Conway, Mila Parely, Naomi Chance, Eric Pohlmann, Andrew Osborne, Richard Wattis, Margaret Halstan, Eileen Way, Michael Ripper.

Paris Model
81 mins
American Pictures Company
Producer: Albert Zugsmith
Director: Alfred E. Green
Screenplay: Robert Smith
Cast: Marilyn Maxwell, Paulette Goddard, Eva Gabor, Barbara Lawrence, Cecil Kellaway, Robert Hutton, Leif Erickson, Tom Conway, Aram Katcher, Florence Bates, Gloria Christian, El Brendel, Michael Romanoff.

1954

Prince Valiant
100 mins
Twentieth Century Fox
Producer: Robert L. Jacks
Director: Henry Hathaway
Screenplay: Dudley Nichols
Cast: James Mason, Janet Leigh, Robert Wagner, Debra Paget, Sterling Hayden, Victor McLaglen, Donald Crisp, Brian Aherne, Barry Jones, Mary Philips, Howard Wendell, Tom Conway.

1955

Barbados Quest
Murder on Approval (US)
70 mins
The Barbour Corporation Ltd
Producer: Robert S. Baker, Monty Berman
Director: Bernard Knowles
Screenplay: Kenneth R. Hayles
Cast: Tom Conway, Delphi Lawrence, Brian Worth, Michael Balfour, Campbell Cotts, John Horsley, Ronan O'Casey, Launce Maraschal.

Breakaway
72 mins
CIPA
Producer: Robert S. Baker, Monty Berman
Director: Henry Cass
Writers: Norman Hudis, Paddy Manning O'Brine
Cast: Tom Conway, Michael Balfour, Honor Blackman, Brian Worth, Bruce Seton, Freddie Mills, Alexander Gauge, John Horsley, Paddy Webster, John Collins.

1956

The She Creature
77 mins
Golden State Productions
Producer: Alex Gordon
Director: Edward L. Cahn
Screenplay: Lou Rusoff
Cast: Chester Morris, Tom Conway, Cathy Downs, Lance Fuller, Ron Randell, Frieda Inescourt, Maria English, Frank Jenks, El Brendal, Paul Dubrov, William Hudson, Flo Bert.

The Last Man to Hang?
75 mins
Association of Cinema Technicians (A.C.T.)
Producer: John W. Gossage
Director: Terence Fisher
Screenplay: Gerald Bullett
Cast: Tom Conway, Elizabeth Sellars, Eunice Grayson, Freda Jackson, Hugh Latimer, Ronald Simpson, Victor Madddern, Anthony Newley.

Copenhagen
15 mins
Hammer Productions
Travelogue
Producer: Michael Carreras
Director: Michael Carreras
Narrator: Tom Conway

Death of a Scoundrel
119 mins
Charles Martin Productions
Producer: Charles Martin
Director: Charles Martin
Writer: Charles Martin
Cast: George Sanders, Yvonne De Carlo, Zsa Zsa Gabor, Victor Jury, Nancy Gates, Coleen Gray, John Hoyt, Lisa Ferraday, Tom Conway, Celia Lovsky.

1957

Operation Murder
66 mins
Danziger Productions Ltd
Producer: Edward J. Danzinger, Harry Lee Danzinger
Director: Ernest Morris
Writer: Brian Clements
Cast: Tom Conway, Sandra Dorne, Patrick Holt, Rosamund John, Robert Ayres, Virginia Kelley, John Stone, Alastair Hunter.

Voodoo Woman
75 mins
American International Pictures (AIP)
Producer: Alex Gordon
Director: Edward L. Cahn
Writers: Russ Bender, V.I. Voss
Cast: Marla English, Tom Conway, Mike Connors, Lance Fuller, Mary Ellen Kay, Paul Dubrov, Martin Wilkins, Norman Willis, Otis Greene, Emmett Smith, Paul Blaisdell.

1959

The Atomic Submarine
72 mins
Gorham Productions
Producer: Alex Gordon
Director: Spencer Gordon Bennett
Writer: Orville H. Hampton
Cast: Arthur Franz, Dick Foran, Brett Halsey, Tom Conway, Paul Dubrov, Bob Steele, Victor Varconi, Joi Lansing.

1960

12 To The Moon
74 mins
Columbia Pictures Corporation
Producer: Thomas E. Fox, Fred Gebhardt
Director: David Bradley
Screenplay: De Witt Bodeen

Cast: Ken Clark, Michl Kobi, Tom Conway, Anthony Dexter, John Wegraph, Robert Montgomery Jr., Phillip Baird, Richard Weber, Muzaffer Tema, Roger Til, Cory Devlin, Anna-Lisa.

1961

The Legend of Mandinga
Documentary
Bardin Productions
Producer: Michael A. Hoey, Britt Lomond
Director: Michael A. Hoey.
Writers: Michael A. Hoey, Britt Lomond
Cast: William Boyett (voice) Tom Conway (voice) Hume Hamilton (himself) Leonid Kinskey (voice) Henry Rowland (voice).

101 Dalmatians
79 mins
Walt Disney Productions
Producer: Walt Disney
Directors: Clyde Geronimi, Hamilton Luske, Wolfgang Reitherman
Story: Bill Peet
Cast: Rod Taylor, J. Pat O'Malley, Betty Lou Gerson, Martha Wentworth, Ben Wright, Cate Bauer, David Frankham, Frederick Worlock, Lisa Davis, Tom Conway, Tudor Owen, George Pelling, Ramsay Hill, Sylvia Marriott, Queenie Leonard, et al.

1964

What a Way to Go!
111 mins
Apjac-Orchard Productions
Producer: Arthur P Jacobs
Director: J. Lee Thompson
Screenplay: Betty Comden, Adolph Green
Cast: Shirley MacLaine, Paul Newman, Robert Mictchum, Dean Martin, Gene Kelly, Robert Cummings, Dick Van Dyke, Reginald Gardiner. Tom Conway (uncredited) Queenie Leonard (uncredited)

Television

The Silver Theatre: *Double Feature*   17/04/1950
The Bigelow Theatre: *Double Feature*   31/12/1950
Bachelor Haven panel show July/August 1951

Mark Saber TV Series (1951 – 1954)

Season One

Date First Aired

05/10/1951	The Case of Carrie's Coffin
12/10/1951	The Case of the Dart of Death
19/10/1951	The Case of the Three Blind Mice
26/10/1951	The Case of the Missing Gun
02/11/1951	The Case of the Toast to Murder
09/11/1951	The Case of the Purse of Death
16/11/1951	The Case of the Silent Alibi
23/11/1951	The Case of the Crown Hill Murder
30/11/1951	The Case of the Vanishing Couple
07/12/1951	The Case of the Living Corpse
14/12/1951	The Case of the Invisible Death
21/12/1951	The Case of the Snowman Murder
28/12/1951	The Case of the Silent Guest
04/01/1952	The Case of the Second Death
11/01/1952	The Case of the Locked Room
18/01/1952	The Case of the Corpse in the Canyon
25/01/1952	The Case of the Finger Man
01/02/1952	The Case of the Fatal Passion
08/02/1952	The Case of the Spirit World
15/02/1952	The Case of the Murder on the Hour
22/02/1952	The Case of the Hidden Clue
29/02/1952	The Case of the Deadly Dream
07/03/1952	The Case of the Missing Heads
21/03/1952	The Case of the Appointment with Death
28/03/1952	The Case of the Idol of Death
04/04/1952	The Case of the Deadly Derringer
11/04/1952	The Case of the Design for Murder
16/04/1952	The Case of the Restless Corpse
23/04/1952	The Case of the Borrowed Corpse
30/04/1952	The Case of the Chinese Medallion
07/05/1952	The Case of the Missing Finger
14/05/1952	The Case of the Haunted Castle

21/05/1952	The Case of the Marked Man
28/05/1952	The Case of the Deadly Queen
04/06/1952	The Case of the Missing Bride
11/06/1952	The Case of the Emigrant of Death
18/06/1952	The Case of the Artful Murders

Second Season

06/10/1952	2.1: Title not known
13/10/1952	The Case of the Star Tattoo
20/10/1952	2.3: Title not known
27/10/1952	The Case of the Hair of the Dog
03/11/1952	The Case of the Wrestler's Corpse
10/11/1952	The Case of the Midnight Murder
17/11/1952	The Case of the Eccentric Heiress
24/11/1952	The Case of the Lost Face
01/12/1952	2.9: Title not known
08/12/1952	The Case of the Murderous Music Box
15/12/1952	The Case of the Mouse
22/12/1952	2.12: Title not known
05/01/1953	The Case of the Fashions of Death
19/01/1953	The Case of the Japanese Knife
02/02/1953	2.15: Title not known
16/02/1953	The Case of the Door of Death
02/03/1953	The Case of the Hanging Husband
16/03/1953	The Case of the Fire of Death
27/04/1953	The Case of the Fatal Ruby
11/05/1953	2.22: Title not known
25/05/1953	The Case of the Triple Murders
Date Unknown	The Case of the Brazen Bride

Other TV Appearances

Assignment Foreign Legion: *The Baroness* Series 1 Ep 2 (1956) George Delacroix

The 20th Century Fox Hour: *Stranger in the Night* Series 2 Ep 2. (1956) Craig Eaton.

Jane Wyman Presents The Fireside Theatre: *Not for Publication* Series 2 Ep 29. (1957) Colonel Coldbrace.

Matinee Theater: *Call it a Day* (S2) (Ep 198) 60 mins. British romantic comedy with Barbara Billingsley 26th July 1957

Alfred Hitchcock Presents: *The Glass Eye* (#3.1) (1957) [Max Collodi]
Cheyenne: *The Conspirators* (3.2) (1957) [George Willis]
Alfred Hitchcock: Suspicion *Rainy Day* (1.10) (1957) [Philip Adams]
Rawhide*: Incident of the Tumblew*eed (1.1) (1959) [Sinclair]
Alfred Hitchcock Presents: *Relative Value* (4.21) (1959) [Inspector]
The Betty Hutton Show: *Goldie Crosses the Tracks* (1.1) (1959)
Tightrope: *The Money Fight* (1.10) (1959) [Nagle]
The Betty Hutton Show: *Goldie Goes Broke* (1.6) (1959) [Seaton]
The Betty Hutton Show: *Art for Goldie's Sake* (1.10) (1959)
The Betty Hutton Show: *Love Comes to Goldie* (1.14) (1960)
The Betty Hutton Show: *Goldie and the Tycoon* (1.18) (1960)
The Betty Hutton Show: *Goldie Gets Amnesia* (1.22) (1960)
The Betty Hutton Show: *The Seaton Story* (1.23) (1960)
The Betty Hutton Show: *Gullible Goldie* (1.26) (1960)
The Betty Hutton Show: *The School Bully* (1.27) (1960)
Alfred Hitchcock Presents: *The Schartz-Metterklume Method* (5.35) (1960) [Mr Wellington] (uncredited)
Adventures in Paradise: *A Penny a Day* Series 2 Ep: 27 (1961)
Have Gun - Will Travel: *The Revenger.* Series 5 Ep: 3 (1961) [Commodore Newcombe]
The Dick Powell Show: T*he Fifth Caller* Series 1 Ep: 13 (1961) [Byron Davies]
Perry Mason: *The Case of the Simple Simon* Series 7 Ep: 24 (1964) [Sir Guy Penrose]

Radio

The Saint

Simon Templar played by Tom Conway

Date Aired

27/05/1951: *The Children's Crusade*
03/06/1951: *The Girl with the Lower Berth*
10/06/1951: *The Funny Man*
17/06/1951: *The Girl Who Had the Midgets*
24/06/1951: *Peter the Great*
01/07/1951: *Death of a Cowboy*
08/07/1951: *Safari's Angels*
15/07/1951: *No, My Darling Daughter*
22/07/1951: *The Big Deal*
29/07/1951: *The Case of the Lop-Sided Triangle*

05/08/1951: *The Perfumed Blonde Case*
12/08/1951: *The Pickpocket Case*
19/08/1951: *A Picture of a Politician*
26/08/1951: *The Prize Fight Case*
02/09/1951: *The Fishing Boat Case*
16/09/1951: *The Round-Robin Murders*
23/09/1951: *The Missing Witness Case*
30/09/1951: *The Baggage Check Case*
07/10/1951: *The Big Shakedown*
14/10/1951: *The Ex-Con Case*
21/10/1951: *The Bracelet*

Sherlock Holmes (Canonical titles in bold type)

Holmes Played by Tom Conway, Dr Watson (Nigel Bruce)

Date Aired

12/10/1946: *The Adventures of the Stuttering Ghost*
19/10/1946: *The Adventures of the Black Angus*
28/10/1946: *The Clue of the Hungry Cat*
02/11/1946: *The Adventure of the Original Hamlet*
09/11/1946: *The Singular Affair of the Dying Schoolboys*
16/11/1946: *The Adventure of the Genuine Guarnarius Aka (The Mystery of the Murdered Violinist)*
23/11/1946: *The Adventure of Sally Martin*
30/11/1946: *The Strange Death of Mrs Abernetty*
07/12/1946: *The Singular Affair of the Coptic Compass*
14/12/1946: *The Adventure of the Elusive Emerald*
21/12/1946: *The Adventure of the Grand Old Man*
28/12/1946: *The Singular Affair of the White Cockerel*
04/01/1947: *The Darlington Substitution*
13/01/1947: THE DEVIL'S FOOT
27/01/1947: *The Singular Case of the Babbling Butler*
03/02/1947: THE DYING DETECTIVE
10/02/1947: *The Strange Case of the Persecuted Millionaire*
17/02/1947: *The Adventure of the Haunted Bagpipes*
24/02/1947: *The Adventure of the Horseless Carriage*
03/03/1947: *Queue for Murder*
10/03/1947: *The Singular Affair of the Ancient Egyptian Curse.* (Tom Conway ill. Ben Wright played Sherlock Holmes)
17/03/1947: THE CREEPING MAN
24/03/1947: *The Adventure of the Scarlet Worm*

31/03/1947: *The Adventure of Maltree Abbey*
07/04/1947: *The Adventure of the Tolling Bell*
14/04/1947: *The Adventure of the Carpathian Horror*
21/04/1947: THE LION'S MANE
28/04/1947: *The Island of Death*
05/05/1947: *The Remarkable Affair of the Pointless Robbery*
12/05/1947: WISTERIA LODGE
19/05/1947: *The Hartley Street Murders*
26/05/1947: *The Adventures of the Submerged Nobleman*
02/06/1947: THE RED-HEADED LEAGUE
09/06/1947: *Murder in the Locked Room*
16/06/1947: *Death in the North Sea*
23/06/1947: THE SPECKLED BAND
30/06/1947: *The Adventure of the Innocent Murderess*
07/07/1947: *The Adventure of the Iron Maid*

Other Radio Appearances

Private Lives: Lawrence Olivier. Vivien Leigh, Tom Conway (Victor). Gulf Screen Guild Theatre 13/10/1940. Tom Conway appearing courtesy of MGM.
Leave it to the People: 15/04/1944 Hollywood Theater
The Hangman: 13/01/1945 Hollywood Theater
Having Wonderful Crime: Old Gold Comedy Theatre. NBC Anthology Series – Tom Conway, Pat O'Brien, June Dupree. 03/06/1945 Hosted by Harold Lloyd.
Brief Encounter: Screen Guild Theater – Irene Dunne, Herbert Marshall, Tom Conway 28/01/1948 (Fred)
Once on a Golden Afternoon: Family Theater – Tom Conway and Natalie Wood 10/06/1948
Once on a Golden Afternoon: Family Theater – Tom Conway and Natalie Wood 02/09/1948
Tom Jones: NBC University Theater – Tom Conway (Tom Jones), Ramsay Hill (narrator) 13/02/1949
The Way of All Flesh: NBC University Theater – Tom Conway (Earnest Pontifax) Ramsay Hill (narrator) 24/04/1949

Recordings

Rob Roy (1954) 'Walt Disney's story of Rob Roy, The Highland Rogue' story told by Tom Conway and Art Gilmore. Music by Billy May. Capitol Records CAS-3198/32137. 10" EP

Works Cited

1. Certified Copy of an Entry of Birth for Thomas Charles Sanders. 15 September 1904, within the district of the British Consulate, St Petersburg, Russia, dated 27 May 1908. See also **GRO Consular Births 1849 - 1965. Vol 12 pg 2840** .

2. **RG32 / Piece 3 / Folio 433.** Miscellaneous Foreign Returns of Births and Baptisms from 1896 to 1910. Thomas Charles Sanders, 4th January 1905. British and American Congregational Church, St Petersburg, Russia. http://www.nationalarchives.gov.uk/doc/open-government-licence/version/2/

3. *Russian Calendar Change*, Rosenburg, J. 20th Century History Guide. Web. 26 Aug 2014. https://www.history1900s.about.com

4. **Gibson, M. H.** *A Bendigonian Abroad.* Bendigo Advertiser, (1855 - 1918) Victoria, Australia, 28 Sep. 1904: 7. Web. 23 Mar 2014. nla.gov.au/nla-news article100525500

5. **Kinross, Albert** . *The Dazzling Spectacle in St Petersburg.* The Catholic Press, Sydney, New South Wales, Australia, 12 May 1904 : 26. Web. 23 Mar 2014. nla.gov.au/nla-news article104895694

6. **Hare, Augustus I. C.** *Studies in Russia.* London : George Allen, 1902. p. 67. Print.

7. **Baskette, Kirtley.** *Hollywoods Most Baffling Bachelor.* New York : Dell Publishing Company, Modern Screen Magazine, June 1941: 44. Print.

8. **Carroll, Harrison.** *Behind The Scenes In Hollywood.* Morning Herald, Uniontown, 15 Nov. 1943: 3. Web. 10 Nov 2012. Ancestry.com.

9. **Welch, Frances.** *The Russian Court at Sea.* London: Short Books, 2011. Print.

10. **John Van der Kiste, Coryne Hall.** *Once a Grand Duchess:Xenia, sister of Nicholas II* : Sutton Publishing Ltd, 2002.

11. *It was a bad toss.* 25 February 1950, The Mail (Adelaide, SA: 1912 - 1954), Austrailia, 25 Feb 1950. 25.Trove. Web. 19 Apr 2014. http://nla.gov.au/nla-news.article58182109.

12. Russia Marriages 1793 - 1919. 11 December 1903. Web. 26 Aug 2013. Familysearch.org.

13. **Vanderbeets, Richard.** *An Exhausted Life.* London : Madison Books, 1990. Print.

14. Russian Births and Baptisms 1755 - 1917. 18 January 1898. Web. 26 Aug 2013. Familysearch.org

15. **Dudley, Fredda.** *The Secret of Sanders.* Screenland Magazine, August 1941, 51. Print.

16. **Mank, Gregory W.** *The Hollywood Hissables.* Michigan : Scarecrow Press, 1989. p. 437.

17. **Aherne, Brian.** *A Dreadful Man.* New York : Simon and Shuster, 1979. Print.

18. **Sanders, George.** *Memoirs of a Professional Cad.* New York : G.P. Putnam, 1960. Print.

19. Border Crossings: from Mexico to U.S 1895 - 1957. Record for Thomas Charles Sanders. 2 Mar 1940. National Archives and Records Administration (NARA), Washington, DC, Record Group:85, Records of the Immigration and Naturalization Service; Microfilm Roll 16.

20. The Independent Record, Helena, Montana. 10 Jun 1953. Web. 19 Apr 2014. Ancestry.com.

21. Russia Births and Baptisms 1755-1917. Record of Christening. Margarethe Jenney Bertha Kolbe. 9 May 1884. Web. FamilySearch(https://familysearch.org) Russia ref p197-28 FHL microfilm 1895619. 20 Jan 2013

22. *Adam Matthew Digital Publications. Order for engine. St Petersburg.* 1834. Reel 174. Web. 15 Sep 2014. http/:www.ampltd.co.uk.

23. *Big Fire at St Petersburg. The Hocking Sentinel (1871-1906), Logan, Ohio.* 27 Sep 1900.

24. *A Disastrous Fire.* Morning Bulletin[Rockhampton, Qld]: 6 Aug. 1912. 7. Web. 17 Sept. 2013. http://nla.gov.au/nla-news.article53272007

25. *An Overview of the Area's Development and Construction History.* Narva Gate OU. Web. 20 Jan 2013 www.narvagate.eu/eng/history.

26. Port of Tallinn. Web. 10 Sept. 2014 www.portoftallinn.com.

27. **Baltic Connections.** Trading Company "Thomas Clayhills & Son". 1633-1944.Web. 26 Aug 2014. http://www.balticconnections.net

28. **Hanway, Jonas.** *An Historical account of the British Trade Over the Caspian Sea, with a Journal of Travels into Persia.* London : 1753. p. 173. Vol. 2.

29. **Conway, Tom**. *My Brother George and I.* Screenland Magazine, December 1942. Print.

30. *Edgar Sanders Comes Home Aka Sandons.* British Pathe, 1953. Web. Britishpathe.com

31. **Kirby, J.** *Bedales School Library and Archive.* Steep, Petersfield, Hampshire, England : 15th Jan 2013. Email correspondence.

32. **H. W. Wilson.** *Year Book.* [ed.] Anna Rothe. New York : 1944. p. 660. Vol. 4.

33. **Brunet, Helen Tower.** *Nellie and Charlie: A Family Memoir of the Gilded Age* : iUniverse, 2005.

34. **Feldman, Robert** *George and his two Gabors.*The Australian Women's Weekly (1932 - 1970), 23 December 1970. p. 5. Web. 16 Oct 2014 http://nla.gov.au/nla.news-article44797674

35. Vladimir Lenin. *Sparknotes.* Web. sparknotes.com.

36. **Foster, Ernest** *Hollywood Film Stop.* The Daily News, Huntingdon. 27 July 1943, p. 7. Web. 04 Dec 2012. Ancestry.com [newspaper database]

37. **Fife, Hamilton.** *My Corners of Armageddon. The London Illustrated News.*1918. p. 309. Vol. 7. Print.

38. **Proctor, Kay.** The New Falcon. *Hollywood Magazine.* February, 1943, Vol. 3, 2, pp. 34 - 35. Web. 21 Aug 2014. Media Digital Library, mediahistoryproject.org.

39. **West, Alice Pardoe.** *Star's Keen Sense of Humor Makes Him Favorite on Lots.* The Ogden Standard Examiner, Ogden, Utah. 25 Apr 1943. Web. 04 Dec 2012. Ancestry.com

40. **Jones, Derek E.** Old Brightonion. *Brighton College.* Web. https://www.brightoncollege.org. 02 Apr 2013.

41. *The Bankruptcy Acts, 1914 and 1926.* The Gazette (London Gazette) 34079. 17 Aug 1934. p. 5312.

42. *Discharge of Bankruptcy,* The Gazette (London Gazette) 34173, 21 Jun 1935, p. 4069.

43. **Encyclopedia Britannica Online - Wikipedia.** Rhodesia. 1922. Web. 2 Apr 2013

44. *Africa Cattle Ranching.* Western Mercury Star, Devon, England, Jan 1921, p. 4.

45. Outgoing Passengers. *Returns of Passengers leaving the United Kingdom in ships bound for places out of Europe, and not within the Mediterranean Sea.* London : The National Archive, London, England, 23 Jun 1923. http://www.nationalarchives.gov.uk/doc/open-government-licence/version/2/

46. *Colonial Report Annual. Northern Rhodesia (1924 - 1925).* London : H M Stationary Office, 1926. p. 5.

47. **Ranger, Terence O.** *Bulawayo Burning: The Social History of a Southern Africa City.* Boydell and Brewer, 2010.

48. *Annual Report on the Social and Economical Progress of the People of Northern Rhodesia.* London : H.M. Stationary Office, 1931.

49. **Board of Trade:Commercial and Statistical Department and successors:Inwards Passenger Lists.The National Archives, Kew, Surrey,**

England. Inward Passenger Lists London : 2nd November 1929. http://www.nationalarchives.gov.uk/doc/open-government-licence/version/2/

50. **Surrey County Council.** *Surrey Electoral Registers* 1939. CC/802/56/3. Surrey History Centre,Woking, Surrey, England.

51. **Lee, Anna, Cooper, Barbara Rosmin and O'Hara, Maureen.** *Memoir of a Career on General Hospital and in film.* McFarland, 2007.

52. **West, Alice Pardoe.** *Actor Tom Conway Would Like Respite From Mystery Roles.* The Ogden Standard-Examiner, Ogden, 30 Oct 1944. p. 11a. Web. 04 Dec 2012. Ancestry.com.

53. **The South Manchester Reporter.** By Dickens we're the oldest Am Dram group in the world. Manchester. 15th April 2010. Web. 19 Apr 2013.

54. *George Sanders' Career.* Northern Star (1875 - 1954), Lismore, NSW, 2 Sept. 1939. p. 6. Web. 19 Apr 2013. http://nla.gov.au/nla.news-article98586907

55. **The National Archives (US).** List Or Manifest of Alien Passengers For The United States Immigrant Inspector of Arrival. San Pedro, California : 6th Sep 1939. Web. Ancestry.com. database.

56. **WRECK SITE.** MV Amerika (+1943). Web 20 Apr 2014. http://www.wrecksite.eu/wreck.aspx?15786.

57. **Dawson, Jack.** *Mystery Man.* Hollywood Magazine, 9 Sept. 1942. Vol. 31. Web. 21 Aug 2014. Media Digital Library, mediahistoryproject.org.

58. **United States of America, Bureau of the Census.** Sixteenth Census of United States Census, Washington D.C.National Archives and Records Administration, 1940. Beverly Hills, Los Angeles, California for Thomas Sanders. Web. 20 Jan 2013. Ancestry.com. database.

59. **Parsons, Louella O.** *Fresno Bee Republican (Fresno, California)* 7 May 1940. Web. 26 Aug 2014. Ancestry.com

60. *A Fine Short Subject.* The Film Daily, 8 Jan 1941. p. 7. Web. 21 Aug 2014. Media Digital Library, mediahistoryproject.org.

61. Advertising The Great Meddler. *The West Australian (Perth, WA:1879 - 1954).* 17 September 1941, p. 7. Web. 10 Oct 2014 http://nla.gov.au/nla.news-article47161174

62. *Brother to a Saint.* Sunday Times (1902-1954), Perth, Western Australia, 23 Feb 1941. p. 8. Web. 07 Sept. 2013. http://nla.gov.au/nla.news-article589624662

63. **National Archives and Records Administration (NARA), Washington, D.C.** *Manifests of Alien Arrivals at Port Huron, Michigan, February 1902-December 1954.* 20 August 1940. Web. Ancestry.com database.

64. **Foster, Carl.** The Strictly Private Life of George Sanders. *Photoplay.* September 1942. Print.

65. *Conway Reveals How He Selected His Stage Name.* Toledo Blade, Toledo, Ohio. 15 Jan 1943. Web. 02 Jan 2013. Ancestry.com. [database]

66. **Fisher, Joe.** Review of the Reviewers. *Edwardsville Intelligencer, Edwardsville, Illinois.* 28th February 1941. Web. 10 Nov 2012. Ancestry.com. [database on-line].

67. *Outstanding Performance.* The Mail, Adelaide, South Australia, 17 May 1941. p. 14. Web. 6 Sept. 2013. http://nla.gov.au/nla.news-article558838317

68. **Parsons, Louella.** Modesto Bee and Herald-News, Modesto, California, 28 Mar 1941. p. 4. Web. 04 Dec 2012. Ancestry.com. [newspaper database]

69. *Televsion of Beauty.* The Coshocton Tribune, Coshocton, Ohio, 9 Mar 1939. p. 7. Web. 20 Jan 2013. Ancestry.com [newspaper database]

70. **Lowrance, Dee.** Priority on Pulcritude. *Montana Standard, Butte, Montana.* 13 December 1942. Web.20 Jan 2013. Ancestry.com [newspaper database]

71. *Tom Conway Goes In For Horrors.* The Milwaukee Journal, Milwaukee, 4 July 1943, p. 4. Web. 10 Nov 2012. Ancestry.com [newspaper database]

72. **Thames, Stephanie.** The Falcon's Brother. Web. *TCM.com.*

73. **Donnelly, Paul.** *Fade to Black:A Book of Movie Obituaries*: Music Sales Group, 2003.

74. **Mank, Gregory W.** *Hollywood Cauldron.* McFarland, 1994.

75. **Fitzgerald, Mike.** Western Clippings. *An interview with Jane Randolph.* Web. 2014. http://www.westernclippings.com

76. **Gabor, Zsa Zsa.** *One Lifetiime Is Not Enough.* [ed.] Wendy Leigh. 1st. New York : Delacorte Press, 1991. p. 148. ISBN:0-385-29882-X. Print.

77. **Allen, Irwen.** *Meet The Stars.* Amarillo Globe, Amarillo, 4 Dec 1942. Web. 04 Dec 2012. Ancestry.com [newspaper database]

78. **TV Radio Mirror.** Tom Conway. March 1954, Vol. 41, 4, p. 304. Web. 21 Aug 2014. Media Digital Library, mediahistoryproject.org.

79. **Fidler, Jimmie.** *Today in Hollywood.* North Adams Transcript, North Adams, Mass, 7 May 1942 p. 18. Web. 04 Dec 2012. Ancestry.com [newspaper database]

80. **Hopper, Hedda.***He Wouldn't Tell.* Berkeley Daily Gazzette, 1942. p. 12 Web. 02 Jan 2013. Ancestry.com [newspaper database]

81. **Johnson, Erskine.** *Anchors Away.* Brownsville Herald, Brownsville, Texas, 20 Nov 1942. p. 4. Web.15 Jan 2013. Ancestry.com [newspaper database]

82. **Fidler, Jimmy.** *Hollywood Roundup.* Evening Standard, Uniontown, Pennsylvania, 23 Dec 1942 p. 6. Web 04 Dec 2012. Ancestry.com [newspaper database]

83. *Reviews of the new films.* The Film Daily. 24 March 1943. Web. 21 Aug 2014. Media Digital Library, mediahistoryproject.org

84. **Fidler, Jimmic.** *Kccp Your Distance.* Nevada State Journal, Reno, Nevada,3 Feb 1943, p. 4. Web. 15 Jan 2013. Ancestry.com [newspaper database]

85. *Tom Can Do Some Detective Work In Own Back Yard.* The Miami News, Miami. 25 May 1943. Web. 04 Dec 2012. Ancestry.com [newspaper database]

86. *Actor Beware.* Pittsburg Post Gazette, Pittsburg. 30 Apr 1943. Web.21 Dec 2012. Ancestry.com [newspaper database]

87. **Fidler, Jimmie.** *Torpedo Boat.*Nevada State Journal, [Reno, Nevada] 12 Mar 1943 Web. 04 Dec 2012. Ancestry.com. [newspaper database]

88. *Chinese Lessons Filmland Vogue.* The Ogden Examiner, Ogden, 25 Apr 1943, p. 14. Web. 4 Dec 2012. Ancestry.com [newspaper database]

89. *He Acts His Age.* TV Radio Mirror. 2, Jul 1958, Vol. 50. Web. 20 Aug 2014. Media Digital Library. mediahistoryproject.org

90. *Reviews of New Films (The Falcon in Danger).*The Film Daily, 20 Jul 1943. Web. 21 Aug 2014. Media Digital Library. mediahistoryproject.org

91. *Odds and Ends.* Lincoln Sunday Journal and Star, Lincoln, Nebraska, 25 Apr 1943, p. 6. Web. 04 Dec 2012. Ancestry.com [newspaper database]

92. **Fidler, Jimmie** *Fidler In Hollywood (Fan Mail).*Nevada State Journal, (Reno, Nevada) 16 [newspaper database] May 1943, p. 4. Web. 10 Nov 2012. Ancestry.com

93. *Tom Conway's Portrayal.* San Antonio Express, (San Antonio, Texas), 18 Apr 1943, p 4. Web. 03 Feb 2013. Ancestry.com. [newspaper database]

94. *Falcon Gets----Yeah, a Falcon!* The Ogden Standard Examiner, Ogden, 2 May 1943, p. 15. Web. 21 Aug 2014. Ancestry.com [newspaper database]

95. *Reviews of New Films (Seventh Victim).* The Film Daily, 24 Aug 1943, p. 6. Web. 21 Aug 2014. Media Digital Library. mediahistoryproject.org.

96. *Kinfolk Make Good In Movies.*   Newcastle Morning Herald and Miners Advocate, Newcastle, N.S.W, 6 Jul 1946, p. 5. Web. 17 Aug 2014. http://nla.gov.au/nla.news-article133159312

97. Border Crossings: From Mexico to U.S. 1895 - 1957. Record card for Thomas C. Sanders. 23 Jul 1943. Web. Ancestry.com database. Note: transcription of original is very poor.

98. *Reviews of the new films (The Falcon and the Co-eds).* The Film Daily, New York, 10 Nov 1943, p. 43. Web. 21 Aug 2014. Media Digital Library. mediahistoryproject.org.

99. *Tom Conway Embarrassed.* Long Beach Independant (Long Beach, California), 17 Oct 1943, p. 33. Web. 27 Jan 2013. Ancestry.com [newspaper database]

100. **Todd, John.** *Director Has Hands Full with These Forty Beauties.* St Petersburg Times, [St Petersburg, Florida], 9 Sep 1943. Web. 26 Jan 2013. Ancestry.com [newspaper database]

101. *His Falcon Role Fits Conway - Almost.* Long Beach Independant, [Long Beach, California], 29 Oct 1943, p. 31. Web. 27 Jan 2013. Ancestry.com [newspaper database]

102. **Fidler, Jimmy.** *Hollywood Roundup (Trouble at Conway Manse).* Evening Standard, [Uniontown, Pennsylvania] 9 Sep 1943, p. 7. Web. 10 Nov 2102. Ancestry.com [newspaper database]

103. *'No separation'.* Pittsburg Post - Gazette, [Pittsburg], 27 Oct 1943, p. Stage and screen page. Web. 10 Nov 2012. Ancestry.com [newspaper database]

104. **Tuska, Jon.** *The Detective in Hollywood.* New York : Doubleday, 1978. p. 243.

107. *Blackie.* Soda Springs Sun, [Soda Springs, Idaho] 4 May 1944. Web. 10 Nov 2012. Ancestry.com [newspaper database]

108. *Reviews of the New Films (The Falcon in Mexico).* New York : The Film Daily, 31 July 1944, p. 7. Web. 21 Aug 2014. Media Digital Library - mediahistoryproject.org

109. *Review (A Night of Adventure).* **The Motion Picture Daily.** 2 Jun 1944, p. 3. Web. 21 Aug 2014. Media Digital Library - mediahistoryproject.org

110. *Detective Conway.* The News (1923-1954), Adelaide, S.A., 10 Feb 1945, p. 5. Web. 7 May 2013. http://nla.gov.au/nla.news-article127294852

111. *Reviews Of the New Films.* **The Film Daily.** 6 Dec 1944. Web. 21 Aug 2014. Media Digital Library - mediahistoryproject.org

112. **Carroll, Harrison** *Is Tom Conway's Face Red!*. Morning Herald, [Uniontown, Pennsylvania], 24 Aug 1944. Web. 27 Jan 2013. Ancestry.com [newspaper database]

113. **Fidler, Jimmy** *Once upon a time.* Nevada Journal, [Reno, Nevada], 10 Oct 1944. Web. 10 Nov 2012. Ancestry.com [newspaper database]

114. **Christian, Lee.** The 11th Annual Film Noir Festival Pays Tribute to Anthony Mann and Ann Rutherford. *American Cinematic League.* [Online] 2009.

115. *Review of the New Films (Two O'clock Courage)* : The Film Daily, New York. 9 Apr 1945, Vol. 87. Web. 21 Aug 2014. Media Digital Library - mediahistoryproject.org

116. **Parsons, Louella.** *Chatter In Hollywood - Tom Conway.* The Lowell Sun, (Lowell, Massachusetts) 17 Feb 1945, p. 11. Web. 21 Dec 2012.. Ancestry.com. [newspaper database]

117. **U.S. Naturalization Record Indexes, 1791 - 1992.** Record for Tom Conway formerly Thomas Charles Sanders, U.S. District Court of Los Angeles, California. 28 June 1946. Web. Ancestry.com database.

118. Licences to import cigarettes. Tobacco. *'Freak explosion'.* Barrier Miner, [Broken Hill, NSW] 11 Jul 1946, p. 6. Web. 16 Oct 2014, http://nla.gov.au/nla.news-article48473845.

119. **Graham, Shelagh.** *Hollywood Today.* Kingsport News, [Kingsport, Texas] 3 Apr 1946. Web. 21 Dec 2012. Ancestry.com [newspaper database]

120. *Hollywood.* 20 April 1946, Dixon Evening Telegraph, [Dixon, Illinois], 20 Apr 1946, p. 4. Web. 10 Nov 2012. Ancestry.com [newspaper database]

121. *Falcon Fighting Biggest Battle – Trying to Escape Playing Detective Roles.* The Milwaukee Journal, [Milwaukee, Wisconsin[, 6 Dec 1946. Web. 04 Dec 2012. Ancestry.com [newspaper database]

122. *Eagle Lion signs Conway.* The Film Daily, New York, 21 June 1946, 120, Vol. 89. Web. 21 Aug 2014. Media Digital Library - mediahistoryproject.org

123. *Hangover Facials For Male Stars.* The Mail, [Adelaide, S.A.], 20 Sep 1947, p. 2. Web. 23 Mar 2014. http://nla.gov.au/nla.news-article55892599

124. *Maybe it s Joke.* Mansfield News Journal, [Mansfield, Ohio,] 16 Jan 1947, p. 23. Web. 10 Nov 2012. Ancestry.com

125. *Sound Men Discuss Problem Stars.* The Mail (1912 - 1954), [Adelaide, S.A.], 24 May 1947, p. 3. Web. 17 Aug 2014. http://nla.gov.au/nla-news-article5585158

126. *Behind the Scenes of Film Production.* Independent Exhibitors Film Bulletin, New York, 6 jan 1947, p. 21. Web. 21 Aug 2014. Media Digital Library - mediahistoryproject.org

127. *The Signals Listening Post.* The Zanesville Signal, [Zanesville, Ohio], 17 May 1947, p. 4. Web. 10 Nov 2012. Ancestry.com

128. *Recommended Listening.* TV Radio Mirror, MacFadden Publications, New York, 6 , 1947, Vol. 27. Web. 21 Aug 2014. Media Digital Library - mediahistoryproject.org

129. **Vale, Virginia**. *Stardust - Stage - Screen - Radio.* The Hopewell Herald, [Hopewell, New Jersey], 15 Jan 1947, p. 7. Web. 26 Jan 2013. Ancestry.com

130. **Bruce, Nigel**. *Nigel Bruce on his new radio partner*. 1, 1998, Sherlock Holmes Journal, Vol. 19.

131. **Fidler, Jimmy.** *Idol Chatter.* The Evening Standard, [Uniontown, Pennsylvania], 29 May 1947. Web. 04 Dec 2012. Ancestry.com

132. **Fidler, Jimmy.** Evening Standard, [Uniontown, Pennsylvania], 17 July 1947, p. 7. Web. 04 Dec 2012. Ancestry.com

133. *George Sanders Sells $10,000 Telescope.* Portland Sunday Telegram and Sunday Press, [Portland, Maine], 11 Sep 1948, p. 8. Web. 10 Nov 2012. Ancestry.com

134. **Fidler, Jimmy.** *Jimmy Fidler in Hollywood (Idol Chatter).* Joplin Globe, [Joplin, Miss], 15 Aug 1947, p. 12. Web. 21 Dec 2012. Ancestry.com

135. **Fidler, Jimmy** *In Hollywood (Out of the Blue).* Pottsdown Mercury and Pottsdam News, [Pottsdown, Pennsylvania], 10 Mar 1947. Web. 10 Nov 2012. Anceestry.com

136. **Hopper, Hedda.** *Looking at Hollywood.* Portland Press Herald, [Portland, Maine], 6 Nov 1948, p. 11. Web. 10 Nov 2012. Ancestry.com

137. *'The Challenge' Well Made Bulldog Drummond Thriller.* **Independent Exhibitors Film Bulletin.** New York, 1948, Vol. 16. Web. 21 Aug 2014. Media Digital Library - mediahistoryproject.org

138. *Reviews (13 Lead Soldiers).* Motion Picture Daily, New York, 28 May 1948, 104, Vol. 63. Web. 21 Aug 2014. Media Digital Library - mediahistoryproject.org

139. *Box Office Slants (13 Lead Soldiers).* **Showmans Trade Review.** 5 June 1948, p. 26. Web. 21 Aug 2014. Media Digital Library - mediahistoryproject.org

140. **Clary, Patricia.** *'Falcon' Star Given Role of 'Biggest Wolf in Hollywood'.* Corpus Christi Times, (Corpus Christi, Texas), 27 May 1948. Web. 04 Dec 2012. Ancestry.com

141. *Bungalow 13 is not a 'B' movie.* Portland Press Herald, [Portland, Main], 27 Nov 1948. Web. 26 Jan 2013. Ancestry.com

142. *Bungalow 13.* Showmen's Trade Review, 27 Nov 1948. Web. 21 Aug 2014. Media Digital Library - mediahistoryproject.org

143. *Review (I Cheated the Law).* **Motion Picture Daily.** 19 Jan 1949, p. 6. Web. 21 Aug 2014. Media Digital Library - mediahistoryproject.org

144. **Parrish, James Robert and Decal, Leonard.** *Hollywood Players: The Forties*: Arlington House Publishers, 1976.

145. **West, Alice Pardoe.** *Behind the Scenes (type cast).* Ogden Examiner, [Ogden, Utah] 3 Jun 1951. Web. 21 Dec 2012. Ancestry.com [newspaper database]

146. **Mason, James.** *Before I Forget* : H.I. Hamilton, 1981. Print.

147. *NBC-TV Pitch for Rights to "Boston Blackie".* Billboard, 6 May 1950.

148. **Entering the Minds Eye.** The Saint. [Online] 2014. http://www.enteringthemindseye.com/thesaint.html.

149. **Siodmak, Curt.** *Wolfman's Maker: memoirs of a Hollywood Writer* : Scarecrow Press, 1997. p. 297.

150. **Gardner, Henry**, Press-Telegram, [Long Beach, California], 13 Jul 1952. Web. 27 Jan 2013. Ancestry.com [newspaper database]

151. **Johnson, Erskine.** *In Hollywood.* Hunbolt Standard, [Eureka, CA], 7 Nov 1952p. 2. Web. 10 Nov 2012. Ancestry.com [newspaper database]

152. The Sunday Star. 9 Nov 1952, *TV Programmes Page.*

153. The Pittsburg Press. [Pittsburg], 8 Jan 1952. Web. 26 Jan 2013. ancestry.com [newspaper database]

154. **Godwin, James.** *The Aylesbury Duck.* Cambridge : Melrose Press, 2006.

155. *Don't Make Yourself a Garbage Can.* South Coast Times and Wollogong Argus, [NSW:1900-1954] 12 Oct 1953, p 7. Supplement Women's Magazine. Web. 16 Oct 2014. http://nla.gov.au/n/a.news-page155555906

156. **British Overseas Airways Corporation.** New York, Passenger Lists, 1820 - 1957. Tom Conway. 12 May 1953. http://search.ancestry.co.uk

157. *Ex Model Asks Actor For Divorce.* Indiana Evening Gazette, Indiana, 16 Jun 1953. Web. 26 Jan 2013. Ancestry.com [newspaper database]

158. Bockley Post - Herald, [Bockley, West Virginia], 22 Jul 1953 p. 4. Web. 21 Dec 2012. Ancestry.com [newspaper database]

159. **Porter, Darwin.** *Those Glamorous Gabors: Bombshells from Budapest* : Danforth Prince, 2013. E.book.(Amazon)

160. NAZIS GETTING MORE CHEEKY. (*SAINT NO SAINT*) **Sunday Mail (Brisbane) (Qld. : 1926 - 1954).** 26 July 1953, p. 4. Web. 16 Oct 2014. http://nla.gov.au/nla.news-article98273854

161. *Wife Sheds Film Actor says He was 'Bachelor'.* Stars and Stripes Newspaper Europe, Mediterranean and North Africa Edition, 26 Ju 1953, p. 5. Web. 10 Nov 2012. Ancestry.com. [newspaper database]

162. **Gwynne, Edith.** *Pottsdown Mercury, [Pottsdown, Pennsylvania],* 15 August 1953. Web. 04 Dec 2012. Ancestry.com [newspaper database]

163. **Graham, Sheilah** *Hollywood Today.* San Antonio Express, *(San Antonio, Texas),* 14 Dec 1953, p. 12. Web. 04 Dec 2012. Ancestry.com. [newspaper database]

164. **Carroll, Harrison.** *Behind the Scenes in Hollywood.* The Lethbridge Herald, *(Lethbridge, Alberta, Canada), 1 Feb 1954,* p. 3. Web. 10 Nov 2012. Ancestry.com

165. *Behind the Scenes in Hollywood.* **Carroll, Harrison.** 9 February 1954, The Lethbridge Herald, [Alberta, Canada], p. 2. Web. 10 Nov 2012 Ancestry.com.

166. **McDougall, Patrick.** *Ramblings of An Also-Ran, Chapter 15.* 2008. Web. debunko.wordpress.com

167. McDougall, Patrick. What was Tom Conway like? 31 January 2013. Email correspondence with author.

168. *Behind the Scenes In Hollywood.* **Carroll, Harrison.** 14 Feb 1955, The Lethbridge Herald, Lethbrige, Alberta, Canada, p. 3. Web. 10 Nov 2012. Ancestry.com

169. *Actor Burned While Filming.* The Bulletin, Glasgow, 29 Mar 1955, No 74, Vol. 40.

170. *Operation on hand* The Bulletin, Glasgow, 31 Mar 1955, Vol. 40, No. 76, p. 3.

171. *Film Stars' Party.* British Pathe, 1955. Web. http://www.britishpathe.com/video/film-stars-party

172. **Guest, Val.** [interv.] Jonathan Rigby: British Film Institute, 5 December 2005.

173. *Stardust - London.* 17th March 1956, Mirror, Perth, [Western Australia: 1921 - 1956], p. 11. Web. 5 Sept. 2013. http://nla.gov.au/nla.news-article75863203

174. **Conway, Tom,** *Film Fanfare No 5. British* Pathe, 1956. Web. Britishpathe.com

175. **Meikle, Denis.** *A History of Horrors: The Rise and Fall of the House of Hammer.* Scarecrow Press, 2008. p. 227.

176. *Film Fanfare 11.* Tom Conway. British Pathe, 1956. Web. Britishpathe.com

177. **Palmer, Randy.** *Paul Blaisdell. Monster Maker: A Biography of the B Movie Makeup and Special Effects.* North Carolina : McFarland, 1997.

178. *Actor Conway in Hospital.* The Stars and Stripes, 6 Aug 1956, p. 5. Web. 10 Nov 2012. Ancestry.com

179. **William H. Brown, Mac Thomas McCrea.** *Fast and Furious: Revised and Fattened fable of American International Producer:* McFarland, 1996.

180. **U.S. National Library of Medicine.** [Online] 2014. http://www.nim.nih.gov.

181. *Tom Conway Operated On.* **The Stars and Stripes.** 5 October 1956. p 6. Web. 30 Oct 2012. Ancestry.com

182. **Parsons, Louella** *Louella Parsons in Hollywood.* 11 February 1957, The Daily Review, Hollywood, CA, p. 18. Web. 10 Nov 2012. Ancestry.com [newspaper database]

183. **Parsons, Louella** *Favorite Hollywood Talk Topics.* San Antonio Light, [San Antonio, Texas], 16 Aug 1959, p. 14. Web.10 Nov 2012. Ancestry.com

184. **Duvoli, John.** *Producer ahead of his time (and budget) yet idle today.* 30 October 1984, The Evening News, Newburgh-Beacon, New York, p. 8B.

185. **Weaver, Tom.** *Eye on Science Fiction:20 Interviews with Classic SF and Horror Filmmakers.* Mcfarland, 2007. Print.

186. *Steaked Out.* The Van Nuys News, Van Nuys, California, 25 Dec 1959, p. 24. Web. 22 Jan 2013. Ancestry.com

187. *Actor's car crashes into parked auto.* Corpus Christi Times, [Corpus Christi, Texas], 6 May 1960, p. 15. Web. 26 Jan 2013. Ancestry.com.

188. *Tom Conway Pleads Innocent to Charge.* Corpus Christi Times, [Corpus Christi, Texas]. 14 May 1960. Web. 26 Jan 2013. Ancestry.com. [newspaper database]

189. *Lost Millions.* Australian Woman's Weekly, 3 Oct 1962. Web. 22 Mar 2013. http://nla.gov.au/nla.news-article43019555

190. *Actor Tom Conway Found Destitute.* The Independant, [Long Beach, California], 14 Sep 1965, pp. A-2. Web. 26 Jan 2013. Ancestry.com. [newspaper database]

191. *Ex Movie Star Conway is Destitute.* Press-Telegram, [Long Beach, California], 14 Sep 1965. p. 9. Web. 22 Jan 2013. Ancestry.com [newspaper databas]

192. **Winchell, Walter.** Eureka Humboltdt Standard, [Eureka, California], 27 Sep 1965. Web. 03 Mar 2013. Ancestry.com [newspaper database]

193. *Remarkably Improved.* The Bridgeport Sunday Post, [Bridgeport, Connecticut], 24 Jul 1966. p. 13. Web. 22 Jan 2013. Ancestry.com

194. *Things are looking up for actor Tom Conway.* The Bridgeport Post, [Bridgeport, Connecticut]. 23 Jan 1967. Web. 22 Jan 2013. Ancestry.com.

195. *Private Rites.* Independent, [Long Beach, California], pp. A-2. 26 Apr 1967. Web. 26 Jan 2013. Ancestry.com

196. The Tyrone Daily Herald, [Tyrone, Pennsylvania]. 13 Mar 1951. p6. Web. 04 Dec 2012. Ancestry.com

197. *Box Office Slant,* Showman's Trade Review, 20 Apr 1946, p 16. Web. 21 Aug 2014. Media Digital Library - mediahistoryproject.org

198. *Things Looking Up For Actor Found On Skid Row,* Corpus Christi Times, [Corpus Christi, Texas]. 23 Jan 1967. Web. 26 Jan 2013. Ancestry.com.

199. *When Good Fellows Get Together*, Photoplay, Nov 1943 Vol. 23 p27. Web. 21 Aug 2014.Media Digital Library - mediahistoryproject.org

200. Project Digest: Reviews. No 1495. Motion Picture Herald, 21 Aug 1943. Web. 21 Aug 2014. Media Digital Library - mediahistoryproject.org

201. *Tom Conway in 'Blue'*, Studio Roundup, Showman's Trade Review, 11 Jan 1947. Web. 07 Sept 2014. Media Digital Library mediahistoryproject.org

202. *It's a Joke, Son!* Premiere Texas Showmanship Event, Showman's Trade Review, 25 Jan 1947, p 22. Web. 23 Oct 2014. Media Digital Library mediahistoryproject.org

203. Hollywood Studio Roundup. Showman's Trade Review, 15 Feb 1947 p 45, Web 23 Oct 2014. Media Digital Library mediahistoryproject.org

204. *RKO's Zombie Launched With Cleveland* Premiere. The Film Daily, 8 Apr 1943 p6. Web. 23 Oct 2014. Media Digital Library mediahistoryproject.org

205. St Petersburg Times [St Petersburg, Florida] 24 Aug 1957.

ABOUT THE AUTHOR

C E Parkinson was born in southern England. After completing an honours degree with The Open University she decided to become a writer. Her first fiction novel, *Tall Shadows, Dark Secrets* was released in 2014 followed by the sequel, *The Camphorwood Chest*, in 2015. She has always had an avid interest in the golden years of Hollywood and enjoyed watching old films from the 1930's and 1940's.

Made in the USA
Columbia, SC
04 May 2025